HE'S NOT THE ONE

The Naked Truth About Dealing With Mr. Wrong

by

V. M. Fowler

APPRECIATION

My special thanks go to the following people:

To all the strong women in my family who have all gone home to be with the Lord: the late Mother Nancy Allen, Evangelist Virgie Ingram, Missionary Annie Branch, my mother Juanita Allen. Thank you all for your love, faithfulness to God, and strength you all displayed to me. Your encouragement, uniqueness, and nurturing down through the years meant the world to me, and I write in portion in your memory.

To my only living mother figure, Pastor Bobbie Brown, I especially thank God for you that from the time our family got the word about my coming into this world you somehow took on the personal responsibility to care for me as if I were your very own daughter. You have been a wonderful role model of God's beauty, love, salvation, forgiveness, and giving. For this I will forever be grateful and indebted to you. You are my angel whom God sent to watch over me.

To the first man of God, (whom I personally accepted as my pastor), non-other than the late great Rev. Samuel J. Smith who was the Founder and Pastor of the Southside Church of God in Christ congregation in Memphis, TN. Being a teenager can bring some pretty tough times coming into puberty, peer pressure, and all types of confusion. I thank God for the foundation Pastor Smith gave us by teaching our Sunday school class every Sunday. We affectionately called him, "Pop." Pop made sure that we all knew God and learned the word of God for ourselves. Pop Smith also made coming to church fun for my age group at the time. He made sure there were youth activities, and Sunday school was fun as well. There was nothing we would not do for Pop Smith because not only did he care about our souls, he cared about our feelings. He knew each and every one of us by name, even by our nicknames. He cared about what we were going through as individuals from different homes. Some kind of way because of Pop Smith I never wanted to miss a church service even during revival week. A lot of pastors today sure could have used the wisdom and knowledge of Pop Smith on building and keeping a congregation strong, and reaching young people in a sanctified yet tangible manner. I want to thank Pop and Mother Smith for being examples of God's love, spiritual leadership, and family.

To Bishop John D. and Pastor Bobbie J. Brown the greatest uncle and aunt in the whole world for always supporting me, and allowing me to be myself. Thank you for allowing me as a saved young adult space and opportunity to serve God in my own way, recognizing my spiritual gifts at a young age, and give me tools to work kingdom building ministry through my calling. You two have shown me that a family that prays together stays together; that husband and wife teaming up can endure anything leaning on God.

Back in 2008 in the O Magazine, Oprah Winfrey asked women to make a magic list of 100 things she wanted in a man. I actually made that list. Can't find that magazine, but I truly believe when I made that list God used my list to create the man of my dreams. The man of my dreams will be everything my healed heart desires. From being a man of God to your height, to your weight, to your wit, to your being so well groomed, to your thoughtfulness, to your honesty, to your attractiveness, to your strong personality, to your youthful flare and the list goes on and on. You are the man of my dreams in so many ways. I dreamed and prayed for a man like you. More importantly, you exemplify Ephesians 5:25-27, "Husbands, love your wives, even as Christ also loved the church, and gave himself for it." You sacrificed and gave so much to prove yourself to me, and my children. I am forever grateful for you doing all you do for me, all of our children, and our entire extended family. I thank you God in advance for sending me Mr. Right some day.

Table of Content

- *2* Appreciation
- *5* Introduction
- *8* A Little About Me
- *13* The Grow Up Plan
- *17* Root Causes
- *20* Life Now vs Life You Want
- *23* When Life Leaves You Broken
- *25* In The Beginning
- *36* Mr Nice Guy
- *47* The Clubbing Ladies Man
- *57* The Preacher's Kid
- *63* Keeping It Real
- *69* I Don't Care Attitude
- *79* The Trap House Thug
- *85* Faith Confession
- *86* Turning to God
- *93* Prayer of Salvation
- *94* Getting a Relationship with God
- *97* 21 Days to Inner Healing
- *98* Remember Your Brothers and Sisters
- *108* The Young Sexy Seducer
- *119* What's Love Got to Do With It?
- *126* Relationship and our History
- *141* Succumbing to Seduction
- *171* There is Hope
- *179* The Awakening
- *186* Possible Red Flags
- *187* The King of Glory Shall Come In

Introduction

"For we wrestle not against flesh and blood, but against principalities, against powers, against the rulers of the darkness of this world, against spiritual wickedness in high places; Wherefore take unto you the whole armour of God, that ye may be able to withstand in the evil day, and having done all, to stand. Praying always with all prayer and supplication in the Spirit, and watching thereunto with all perseverance and supplication for all saints." **_Ephesians 6:12-18_**

My name is Ms. V and I wrote this book for every woman, especially church girls; who have had trouble choosing the right type of man. I wrote this book for every woman who grew up without a father or father figure. I wrote this book for every young girl out there who feels like no one loves you, or that you are not worth much. I wrote this book for every young lady out there who had a man tell you, "Well if you love me then you would …." I wrote this book for every woman out there who has been made to feel that if you don't put out then a man will not put up with you. I wrote this book for ever woman who said no, but the man did it anyway. This book is for every woman young and old to help you realize that you are never alone or the lone rider in your situation. For you who grew up not being taught by your parents about boys and sex, and had to figure it out by looking at magazines, movies, and listening to young and dumb friends. There have been many before you, and there will be many after you going through your same tests and trials. Feeling unloved, unwanted, or unsuccessful are just some of the tricks and the fiery darts that the enemy throws our way. **_Romans 6:10-18_** teaches us that after everything good, bad, and ugly that we have ever gone through.... that after all that, having a cultivated prayer life and intimate relationship with God makes a big difference with us staying in undesirable situations or moving on into a new happy life. See, what I have learned, my dear sister, is that when you are born into a crazy family and world of drama, dysfunction, ignorance, and trouble.... then you must realize that God created you to be different; the exact opposite of them. Oh no! God has created you to be born to be a person who will affect and bring change to a dying world here on earth. You were created to be a holy vessel of God's glory and love in the earth; to flourish with all blessings and prosperity. *"Ye have not chosen men, but I have chosen you, and ordained you, that ye should go and bring forth fruit, and that your fruit should remain: that whatsoever ye shall ask of the Father in my (Jesus) name, he (God the father) may give it you"* **John 15:16**. See, we do not get the luxury of choosing the family or circumstances we are born into, BUT we do get the chance to choose how our life will develop and eventually end up.

A Little About Me

I have lived most of my life trying to either be loved by others, accepted by others, be what others wanted me to be, or just be a part of the in crowd. You are here reading this book, and probably just like me. But it's okay because just like me, you will gain wisdom day by day and are gonna be just fine.

Growing up there were so many things that happened to and around me which forced me to suffer in silence in order to cope and deal with all the craziness; well, some of the time. Most of the time, I just checked out into my own imaginary world of pretending with my dolls of having a better life, or reading and writing stories. Mostly of the time I wrote to God. Most of the time I forced myself to smile instead of cry. Most of the time I had to go to a place in my mind which made me strong enough to get through the hurt that was happening to me in that moment. Most of the time, there was absolutely no one I could trust, no one I could confide in, no one I could talk to, no one who could help. I felt helpless, unloved, unwanted, and doomed. In spite of all of the good people around me showing me love, I could not see the forest for the tree. Why? Because I wanted that love and support from those I chose to want it from. I walked around believing that if I loved them and treated them nice then they would return the favor. Things got so bad emotionally for me, that I began to believe that I really just wanted to die. I mean, with the way I was being treated, surely there was no reason why I should be here. Did God make a mistake? Did God really mean for me to be alive? Did God have a purpose or plan for me? If so, what is the plan? These were just some of the questions which toiled me as a child growing up. Do you feel this way at times? Do you ask yourself some of the same questions? Do you sometimes wake up feeling like you just wanna run away or end it all? Well, so did I for the dark season in my life until I found Jesus and a better understanding about communicating with God.

It was okay to hang out and talk with family and friends, but I never felt completely comfortable with telling anyone what was going on with me. Then one day I found hope in God by writing out my thoughts. I found out there is a reason for everything under the sun, and learned that all things work together for good of them who love the Lord. More important, I found out that when you talk to God whether through singing, praying, writing or flat out talking, He actually talks back to you. Singing to God is my best communication with Him because I get to worship Him and tell Him how great of a God He is to me. He has been my closest friend, confidant, and provider. Plus, When I feel discouraged, insecure, or scared God has a way of giving me hope and strength; picking me up and reassuring me through His word that I am loved and gonna make it through whatever it is I am going through because I have a purpose. But, what was my purpose? What was the reason little ole me was born? Why should I stay here, and live out my life? You probably ask yourself the same questions. Take it from me, if you start asking God about it He will definitely reveal and manifest His blessings and purpose for your life. I am telling you that no matter what the problem is, or no matter how people hurt you or mistreat you, or life disappoints you; no matter what comes your way these battles are just check points in your personal spiritual boot camp. God will allow people and situations to come into your life, just like He did in the bible with Job, and watch you learn about yourself and grow. There is a part we can own in every bad situation that we can use to learn and grow. Life is tremendously amazing and unpredictable at times, but the more we lean on God and learn of His word we grow in discernment, knowledge, understanding and wisdom. But we must learn with God. We must get with God about every situation, and ask him to help us and show us the way. This is what I have learned to do, and now my life is truly peaceful and happy. It may take you years and years of going through the same thing over and over again, but eventually as you keep conditioning your spiritual muscles and getting spiritually fit soon your past will actually be your past, not your present, and your future will be on the path to the right destination of favor and abundance. God is no respecter of persons; meaning what He has done for one He can and will do for all. But only if we tap into His word, learn His voice, and learn to discern His will for every answer we seek.

The Grow Up Plan

It is amazing how life starts out. As a new born, you don't have a care in the world. Then, your senses are awakened, and you figure out who cares for you. This is usually mom or dad or some other family member, but you begin to have a sense of comfort for those who do care for you. Life is grand, until you learn there are boundaries, and people are not always so pleasant and care for you. This can make a child feel confused and scared. It is where critical thinking really starts.

See, I learned from a young age that hate, harm, and hurt comes from the people you least expect it from. As a child you depend on the adults around you to protect, and care for you. Unfortunately, everybody doesn't love you or even like you. Even down to your family and parents, they may hate or resent you. It is not because they woke up one day and decided to be this way, but because of all the hurt and heartbreak they have gone through in their life. An easy way to forgive them is to accept this wisdom that people do the best they can do with what they are working with. People love you the best way they know how. Whether they know better or not, it may not be in their mental or emotional capability to love you or treat you the way God intended them to. It does not mean that you are less deserving, or that you will never be loved or treated in the manner you deserve. It just means that you may never get that love and acceptance from those you expect it from the most. You know what I have learned over the years? We waste far too much time crying, complaining and dwelling on our problems instead of focusing on solutions. God places so many people and situations in our path for us to get all the blessings, love and support we need, but we miss them all, and let them all go because we are blinded by our deep emotional hurt which causes us to only see people and situations as the problem.

Start looking around and find out who God has placed around you to be a loving, positive support to you, and stop taking them for granted before it is too late and they are gone. It is time to grow up and start appreciating all the good people and opportunities God has given you before you lose them; before you are left with your bitterness, hurt, and those who keep you in that vicious cycle. Stop giving the devil a foot hole in your life to wreak havoc and keep you down. Start attending church at least twice a week. Join a team at your church where you can serve and connect with some good people. Pray and study your word every day. Listen to nothing but gospel music for 21 days. Welcome the Holy Spirit into your heart and your life every single day through song and worship. Acknowledge God in all your ways, and He shall direct your path into being a path full of abundance, favor, and miracles. I am a living witness that if you try it for at least 21 days your life will transform and never be the same.

Your life will be so much better, so much so that you will keep repeating those 21 days to keep yourself flowing in the blessings of God and His peace. Growing up is not all about the bad things that happen along the way, but more about how you draw closer to God and learn and grown into a better person having a better life.

There are many, like myself, which have grown up with a mixture of treatment from adults and caregivers. Some people are nice, but many can be just downright cruel. There is no excuse for mistreatment or abuse of any child or person even though it happens every day. The country of the land of the free and home of the brave is full of terror for so many children and adults. What I have learned is my short life is that without God, we can be literally brought down to nothing, but with God we can ALWAYS rise up in triumph. To God be the glory for all the things he has done in my life, and what he is about to do for you.

Root Causes

There is something I found out to be the cold hard truth about myself, and everyone else in the world. There is a root cause to everything we say and do, and when our roots have a blue print of improper or dysfunctional experiences then we are shaped into improper and dysfunctional people. Something happened early on or at some point in our lives to affect us. Something happened to influence us. Something happened to teach us to be who we are today. Something happened to condition us. Something happened to make us think and act the way we do; every single bit of us has been formed from childhood experiences. Some of us build off of those experiences, and branch of into what some call the reinvention of oneself, but some of us build off of those experiences, and allow ourselves to get trapped into the same common demise that we said we would make sure when we grow up we would escape out of all because we do not realize how wrong we are. And when you don't know, you just don't know. At some point I had to decide what I wanted and who I wanted to be in life. I wanted to know better so I could do better. I said to myself, if there is a God there has got to be a better life and situation for me.

Have you ever wondered or asked yourself, "Why is it that I think this way?" or "Why is it that I believe that way?" or "Why do I always fall for this or that?" Have you ever wondered why you are the way you are, feel the way you feel, or love the way you love? How about the way you walk, and how you talk? What about the kind of places you like to hang out in, or the types of people you like to hang around? What about how educated you are, or not? Do you like the finer things in life or knock offs? I mean really who are you? Who do you really want to be? **Proverbs 23:7** teaches us *"For as a man thinketh in his heart, so is he."* Is your life as good as it gets, or is there something better? If life is bad for you I am here to tell you that there is better out there for you. God has not given us life to die miserable and alone in this world. God says in His word, that "He wishes above all things that we will prosper and be in good health even as our souls prosper" **3 John 1:2**. As a matter of fact God has blessed us to be a blessing; the head and not the tail; above and not beneath; the lender and not the borrower. This is the will of God concerning you. Not the bad things or the bad people the devil has used to kill, steal, and destroy your good life. You feel me? You rise up and tell Satan that **Jesus died so that I might live**, so get thee behind me!

Life Now vs. The Life You Want

Every thought

Every feeling

Every action

Every belief

…that you have, comes from a part of your soul; your blue print which has been nurtured, mentored, tortured, beaten, or built on a certain foundation instilled in you from birth and through every single experience in life.

I want to get you to think about your life and lifestyle; your quality of life now vs what you want. Then read **Psalm 1:1-6** daily. It reads, *"Blessed is the man that walketh not in the counsel of the ungodly, nor standeth in the way of sinners, nor sitteth in the seat of the scornful. But his delight is in the law of the Lord; and in his law doth he meditate day and night. And he shall be like a tree planted by the rivers of water, that bringeth forth his fruit in his season; his leaf also* *shall not wither; and whatsoever he doeth shall prosper."* Also read **Jeremiah 17:7-8**, *"Blessed is the man that trusteth in the Lord, and whose hope the Lord is. For he shall be as a tree planted by the waters, and that spreadeth out her roots by the river, and shall not see when heat cometh, but her leaf shall be green; and shall not be careful in the year of drought, neither shall ceased from yielding fruit."* I challenge your mind and spirit to consider this: "IF YOUR CURRENT SITUATION OR CONDITION OR STATUS IS JACKED UP AND NOT WORKING WELL FOR YOU AND YOU WANT A BETTER LIFE, THEN IT IS TIME TO FACE ONE OF YOUR BIGGEST FEARS > ROOT CAUSES > **CHANGE**.

Focus
On
Change
Until
Success

Your Mindset

Change, ***Focus***, and ***Rebirth*** are all accomplished through the knowledge and understanding we gain by studying the word of God after our life experiences. Not only does God expect us to study it, but He also expects us to live by it. We can only find the truth about any matter by getting with God and studying His word. **James 1:22** *"But be ye doers of the word, and not hearers only, deceiving your own selves."* Yes, God holds us all accountable for our own quality of life because who we are and who we want to be is not to be left to chance, but it is a matter of our choice. Do you want to stay where you are, or choose something better? There is a better life waiting for you to get at it. Start today by applying the 21 day process. I am witness that it will change your life for the better. No, life will not be perfect, but you will have more peace and blessings in your life. This is not something I was told, it is something I have tried and tested for myself, and found it works.

When Life Leaves You Broken

There was a time in my life when I was under some extremely adamant stress. I mean, it was to the point where I could absolutely go no further in life without some form of proper counseling. See, when you get so broken, and filled up with pain you will bleed through the wounds of your past until you heal. You may begin to use things like alcohol, drugs, food, work, or sex; but eventually, all of your pain will ooze out through the crevices of your heart and spill over into your life causing you to break down or give up. None of these devices will cure your problems or take your pain away. **You** must find strength and courage to tend to your wounds, and get to the core of the painful memories of your past to make peace with them. The way that I did it was first through therapy intervention. Then, I added God to the equation, and He made it alright. Read **Psalm 34**, but pay attention to the verse 18, *"The Lord is nigh unto them that are of a broken heart; and saveth such as be of a contrite spirit."* You can try everything out here in these streets, but when you get to a place where you are so tired that you are broken, when you get to that broken place this is where God can really work on you and your situation. Why? Because in your broken place you will cry out to God, and you will be willing to do whatever it takes to surrender your all to Him; and give God complete control over your life through hearing and doing his Word. I tell you, we sing about it in our choirs, but it is true. When Jesus comes all of Satan's power is BROKEN. The blood still works!

WARNING: The next part of the book will be some real stories about what different types of relationships look like. Some people and places are fictitious to keep them anonymous. It gets real, so you can choose to stop reading at this point. Read on at your own risk.

"Train up a child in the way he should go: and when he is old, he will not depart from it." **Proverbs 22:6**

In The Beginning

Now, I was born and raised in Memphis, TN. My earliest memories as a little girl are living in the Lemoyne Owen Gardens. It was the projects, but they have since been torn down. There were the next door neighbors, my best friend Kay Kay and her family, then my aunt's friend, her mom, Ms.

Katherine, who lived a few doors down, Ms. Bea the neighborhood candy lady, the people across the way with all these kids, and the lady who lived next door or maybe a couple doors down who always had all these dead cock roaches in her apartment. I remember our family was close. I had aunts, my grandmother, and me who all lived together in this 3 bedroom apartment. Or was it a 2 bedroom apartment?

The years I spent there as a child were awesome. I remember always playing outside, only coming in to go to the bathroom, get something to drink, or to eat. Back then, life was so carefree. There was always food on the table. We may have been poor living in the projects, but it seemed like we were rich. My grandmother was very spiritual, and she always made sure we were going to church. Yes, Nancy Allen, my grandmother, did not play when it came to church. You know, I think back then black people went to church so much because there were not many places we could go for fun or entertainment other than a juke joint or house party. Going to church was one of my family's favorite pastimes.

What I loved as a small child was the feeling and sense of family. There was always someone around, watching, caring, and making sure you were alright. It was truly about a village raising the children. When my friends and I were outside playing, if we were doing anything wrong, or getting in someone's yard we were not supposed to, there was always some nosy neighbor calling out to us telling us to behave. Yeah, back then you knew that you could not get away with much because if the neighbor caught you, then your family and the rest of the neighbors would know about it. As if that was not bad enough, after the neighbors got finished scolding you about what you have done wrong, then you had to wait until your family gets home then ALL of them would get on you to. Back then, the neighbors would spank you, then your mom would spank you, grandma, aunts, and on down the list.

I bet I was good for a good month when I got in trouble for the least little thing, but I don't remember getting into too much trouble myself. I might have been around kids cutting up, you know, a bystander, accessory to the crime (laughing).

I guess pretty much we were sort of poor, because my friends and I would play in dirt a lot, and catch June bugs and lightening bugs. We would somehow catch the June bugs, tie one of their legs to a string, and run with them as they were flying attached to the string; like it was a kite. The thought never occurred that it might have hurt the June bugs to be played with like that, but we got such a big kick out of it. I remember laughing so loud, running, jumping, and playing. And we would make mud pies, and put mud on our face. Guess this was the original face painting, but none of the adults liked it. They seemed to get all uptight when we had to come inside all dirty. I never got spanked for playing outside. It seemed my family was willing to endure all the dirt, cuts and scrapes, and bumps and bruises I would get while playing outside from dawn to dusk. Where did those days go? Nowadays, it is hard to find a bunch of kids just playing outside together; well up north anyway.

Let me tell you about some of the characters in our neighborhood back then. First, it was Kay Kay and her family. Their home was always neat like ours, and they always had good snacks to. It was her mom, her brother, and herself. I do not remember them having a father. They could have had one, but I just don't recollect them having a man living with them. I believed Kay Kay had an older brother who was away in college. It was a grand reception when he would come home. As a matter of fact when any of the project families had a son who went away to the military or college there was always a big party thrown when they came home. Those were the nights we got to stay up with the adults, and have fun until late at night. Kay Kay was my best friend though. Even though she was older, she treated me like her little sister, and always played with me. I remember we would sit outside at night at the table in their yard and our yard, and listen to music and talk and laugh. She or someone else would braid my hair, and she loved talking about boys. I was not at the age of talking about boys though because I thought boys were the worst at my age. If Kay Kay had to go to school or somewhere else, I would be right there waiting for her to return home to spend time with me. I loved Kay Kay and used to wish she was my real sister. Wonder whatever happened to Kay Kay.

Then there is my grandmother's good friend, and church partner, Ms. Bea. We called my grandmother Mama. Well at least I did because my aunts called her Mama. Anyway, it seems every day Mama and I would go down to Ms. Bea's home for a visit. Sometimes there would be other women there sitting around eating, and chatting about all kinds of stuff like the neighborhood gossip, or something happening at the church. These ladies were funny, but got on my nerves at the same time. I remember being so glad to dart out of the door to go outside and play while Mama was visiting with Ms. Bea. I don't remember Ms. Bea having a husband or man around either. Matter of fact, it seems no one hardly had a man around. Well, sometimes they would have boyfriends I guess who would visit from time to time, but really there were not a lot of men who lived in the projects with us. Anyway, Ms. Bea used to sell candy, and other items. My favorites were the vanilla wafers, soft chew peppermint sticks, pickles, and pickled pigs feet. Yes, I used to eat pickled pigs feet. Man, I used to tear those things up (laughing). Can't get me to eat em today, but back then I used to lick my fingers to the bone going in on some pickled pigs feet. See, we did not go many places outside of the neighborhood. I remember, we were almost always home around the neighborhood. Maybe on the weekends, or special occasions we would dress up and go to the Woolworth, or Sears and Roebuck, but for the most part we would mostly be at home and eat at home. Maybe the reason why we needed a candy lady is because it was safer. We went to the neighbors for everything like borrow stuff, and stayed around the home front so much is because it was dangerous to go out to places. I remember, I would think about it a lot. You know… the reason why we only visited places and people we knew. There were times I saw mistreatment, and racism happening, but I did not know what it was at the time. I just thought people always fought, or white people were mean. Anyway, I was cool with going to Ms. Bea's home because her home was like ours, clean and bug free.

Then there was Ms. Katherine's home. Now I used to like going to Ms. Katherine's home, but there was just one question that bothered me. Why is all Ms. Katherine's furniture covered in plastic? (laughing) Her home was very neat also, but her living room looked like something out of a Hollywood movie or something. It was like we should have been dining with the president or a fine ladies society at her place. My aunts would visit with Ms. Katherine's daughter, and take me with them I guess to give Mama a break or because they were watching me. Seems like every time we went to Ms. Katherine's house it was my aunts or one of my aunt's and Ms. Katherine's daughter sitting in the kitchen while she did laundry and pressed clothes. I was like why we have to always come down here when this lady is doing laundry in the kitchen. Guess that was their favorite pastime. Maybe my aunts liked to keep Ms. Katherine's daughter company while she did her laundry. And they would be talking about all kinds of gossip, and the men they were dating. They had good snacks and food also. I guess the way to keep me quiet was to give me something to eat, and set me down to watch TV while they had their ladies visit for girl talk. It was Ms. Katherine and her daughter who lived I their home. There wasn't a man there either. Ms. Katherine was so sweet though, and calm. I like her home because it was neat and peaceful accept for the kitchen on laundry days (laughing).

Now, the way our neighborhood was set up, the backyards to the buildings were facing each other with a sidewalk separating a row of homes on each side of the sidewalk. Each backyard was separated from the next door backyard with a sidewalk leading up to a step to the back door. Everyone's yard was different. Our yard really did not have much in it, but Kay Kay's and her family's yard had a picnic table. Everyone used to come over to Kay Kay's family's home to sit out, barbeque, and listen to music or play cards. I used to be sort of proud to live next door to Kay Kay and her family. But then directly across from our home was the lady with so many children she did not know what to do. Yeah, like the lady in the shoe.

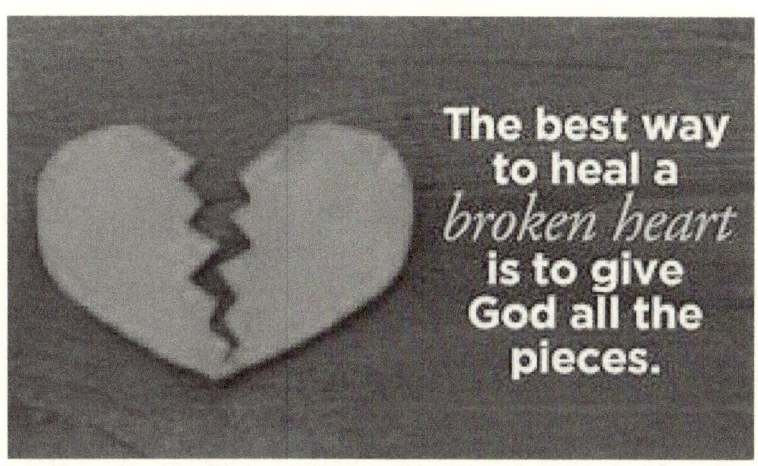

"Let no man despise thy youth; but be thou an example of the believers, in word, in conversation, in charity, in spirit, in faith, in purity." **_1 Timothy 4:12_**

Mr. Nice Guy

I must say, it is true that I fall hard when I fall in love with someone. From the beginning, when I started liking boys, I used to always dream of getting married, and living happily ever after with my knight in shining armor. The dream continued with us having four children, two boys and two girls; having college degrees, the best money making careers, and a big house with every amenity, and let me not forget to mention the white picket fence which was a must. A girl be tripping when she is young, and full of dreams. I would constantly think about my man taking me in his arms, dancing with me, and taking me out on regular dates; making me feel like I was his queen and his world. After about twenty years or so, this dream came to a screeching stop. There was **no** college degree, **no** marriage, **no** knight in shining armor, **no** children, and definitely **no** house with a white picket fence. Yeah, I had to get my mind straight, and step into reality that the time clock was ticking. I did not give up so easily, as you can see, and not before having a valiant attempt in life at trying to have a relationship with several men.

It all started with Mr. Nice Guy, Edmond. See Edmund was this funny looking dude, with what seemed like the perfect family. It was back in my middle school days when I noticed boys were checking me out, but I was so super shy, a virgin, and not allowed to really date. There were so many guys I had a crush on, but only one guy was persistent in trying to give me respect, and impress me. That guy was Mr. Edmond. He went to my church, so we saw each other multiple times each week. We had a hanging out click back in the days, and we all went to the same church. Almost every Sunday night or Friday night during or after church we would all try to hang out together. This crew was so much fun, and of course there were those in our little click who acted more grown up than they probably should have. I remember two of the girls were sisters, and we all loved to hang out at their house. See, they had a big screen television and cable. But, getting back to my crushes, I had a crush on two boys at the time, one named Jay and the other Big D. Now Big D was so distinguished looking, and it seemed every girl wanted him. I guess you can say he was out of my league, and the catch of the town. Nevertheless, I used to be checking him out like every time I saw him. Then there was Jay. Man, this guy was so charming, but he really wasn't about nothing back then. We got close and I would even spend the night at his mom's pretending to be a tag along to babysit or go to church with her. They lived not too far from my Aunt Angel, so even if I did not want to spend the night with Jay and his mom I would just walk over there and hang out with Jay. Then one day it happened. All of Jay's messing around came back and bit him in the butt. Jay had a baby with some girl. I was shocked, and heartbroken. I mean even though he was not about much, he was fine and was a great friend. We always had fun together, until he started having baby mama drama. I mean the girl would pull up, mouth wide open talking junk. Sometimes Jay's mom would be just standing there in shock, with her jaw dropped like it was the first time she ever seen the baby's mom in action. Way too much drama, so I quickly dissolved my crush on Jay. He moved away right after he graduated from high school.

Then there was Big D; tall, dark, and drop dead gorgeous. He looked like something out of the GQ Magazine. He was always dressed sharp from head to toe. Yeah, somebody taught that boy how to wear swag even back then. He used to mainly play the drums instead of singing in the choir with the rest of us. He was a hot item with his girlfriend, Tiera. Tiera had a reputation though. It was said that she slept around with mad boys, but that did not stop Big D from being in love with her, and defending her honor. I mean even though she did not have much to honor from the rumors, but he was head over heels for her. I used to be like what in the world did she do to keep him chasing her. I remember, though, at some point Big D and Tiera broke up. After that Big D came to visit me a couple times. He even took me out. Once when he was over to my house we were sitting on my couch close. He did the whole arm around and scoot move on me. You know when the guy swings his arm around you, then scoots closer to you on the sly. He was so close I was a bag of nerves inside. I could even hear my heart beating so loudly in my head as if it was gonna jump out. But, this day, Big D put the smack down on me. He kissed me ever so gently and passionately. Something went through my whole body. I remember feeling faint, and thinking this boy cannot come over here again because I might get pregnant kissing like this. I really did not know how to kiss, or that you could not get pregnant from just kissing. That was back in the days.

I want to take some time right here to speak to the ladies both young and mature. It does not matter if you are eighteen or eighty-two. If you are with a man, but you are not happy there are two things you first need to figure out: #1 Is it you? #2 Is it him? See, maybe you just got with him for all the wrong reasons. Maybe it is vice versa, and he only got with you for the wrong reasons. Either way, when you hook up with someone and the true intentions are not pure or innocent; problems can begin to set in with frequent occurrences of confrontational events which ultimately will cause the relationship to fail. Once you figure this mystery out, then you have about half your battle of having an unproductive relationship solved.

Take Edmond for instance. We grew up in the early 80's as teenagers in the Church of God in Christ. Yes, the C.O.G.I.C, where we sang our church song, "We try to do what's right, in and out of sight, here at Southside Church of

God in Christ." Man, those were the days. Talking about real church, and serving God. Oh, our pastor did not play, and the ushers and mothers of the church did not play either. I remember they tried to get all of us young folk saved every summer it seemed. Then the renowned Evangelist Darrell Hines would come run revival. He was awesome, and about the most amazing preacher I had ever heard. Plus, he could sing, dress, and when the preaching got good he would sort of rare back, microphone in the air with his hands on his hips. I remember feeling so important singing in the choir in that little ole church especially when Evangelist Hines came into town to do revival. But the altar calls and tarrying services were hilarious. I mean we would all go down to the altar, knee while different ministers and deacons and missionaries would basically be yelling their hot funky breath in our faces. It was torture. This would go on for what seemed like an eternity either until somebody got tired, or it was time for the benediction. We would laugh and joke about who got saved all over again, but sometimes it would get real serious, and we would get touched by the Holy Spirit for real.

Anyway, back to Edmond. Edmond ended up being my best friend, and what we called my church boyfriend because we mostly only saw each other in church or after church. Everybody would couple off and sit together during the church services. Kind of a neat set up in case you were not allowed to really date like I was. Well, Edmond was such a fine young man. We both had our first kiss with one another. He always took such good care of me, but then there was just one big issue; his mother did not like me at all, and she eventually let me know in so many words. She was downright mean to me. After she pulled me to the side one day, and let me know how she felt about me, I was so hurt and torn. I never looked at Edmond and his family quite the same after that. Did not change the love I had for his father, sisters, and grandmother. In fact, I loved going home with them after church for Sunday dinners. So long story short, I ended up moving away to New Jersey the day after my high school graduation without even telling Edmond. It broke my heart to know someone who meant the world to me had a family who would never truly accept me. I knew how much he loved his mother, so I could not bring myself to tell him why or what I was feeling because I knew he would have probably loved me anyway. He gave me unconditional love and friendship, but I just did not want to ruin his family, or come between him and his mother.

Edmond was my first attempt at a love relationship. I became the problem, though, because I did not communicate to my man my thoughts and feelings. I did not give love a chance. About a year later, I came back home to Memphis, and reunited with Edmond. Can you believe he still loved and cared for me, but so much had happened in my life that what I believed I needed from him, he was incapable of giving to me at that time. I wanted him to marry me, and take care of me, and be my super hero so to speak. I was in a serious homeless situation, so I had enlisted in the United States Air Force thinking I was too much of a problem to anyone, and would hold him back. So, I pretended I believed it would not work, and never saw Edmond again even though he urged me to not give up on us being together and helping one another. My first true love, and probably would have been the best man forever in my life, just like his father was to his family. To have never been with another boy or man who loved and cared for me so much made it very painful for me to let Edmond go. For the longest I wanted so much to have another guy in my life as healthy both emotionally and spiritually as Edmond to love me. He loved me so unselfishly and unconditionally like no one else had done other than my grandmother and favorite aunt. To this day I regret not having enough knowledge and maturity to express myself; not enough courage to stand up for myself and just tell Edmond what was going on and how I really felt about him and how I wanted to trust the love he had for me and that I had enough to give him back in return. Well, just like always I ran away from that situation, and ran right into the hands of Satan. Not long after moving to NJ I met a ratchet guy named Paul.

A FIRST KISS MAY BE WITH A GUY WHO WILL NOT BE YOUR LAST KISS.

V.M. Fowler

"Flee also youthful lusts: but follow righteousness, faith, charity, peace, with them that call on the Lord out of a pure heart." **2 Timothy 2:22**

The Clubbing Ladies Man

Did I mention I was still a virgin all the way through high school until graduation? Yes, I was a virgin until I moved to New Jersey, and met this clubbing and dance crazed guy named Paul. Paul had a crazy family to; a mean sister, a brother in jail, a drinking father, and a sweet mother who was the rock of the family. He had other brothers and sisters to who visited often to check on mom and dad. I had never had seen a more loving and dedicated mother, and wife than this woman. This woman would work her fingers to the bone preparing and selling dinners every week to raise money to help to get her son out of jail or help with attorney fees. Paul was a ladies' man. I used to get all kinds of females approaching me about him especially at work. My job was in the gift wrap department at Macy's in the Quaker bridge Mall. Some chick was always trying to make me jealous, asking me questions; talking about how Paul would be hanging out in clubs dancing, etc. in the Zanza Bar. Paul would not take me out dancing, instead we would spend time at his mom's house, going out to eat, or to the movies. But at midnight (because I had a curfew) he would get me back home on time then go hang out at the club hopping friends. I sort of envied them because there was no way the house of prayer lords, my aunt and uncle, would even think about allowing me out past midnight, and everyone knows that the party doesn't get started until midnight. So I was told back then. So I learned after going to my first party much later in life.

Getting back to Paul, one night I got the chance to spend the night with one of my girlfriends, so we decided to go and spy watch for Paul at the Zanza Bar Club. We sat there until we saw him come out. He was all hugged up with some female. You already know it went down, but I remember telling him it was over between us then getting in my car and leaving. I had been through so much with him, but I gave him one more shot. See, I should have ended the relationship the night he deflowered me. Yes, Paul was the chosen one; my first. He would always try to pressure me about sex, but I did not want to until marriage. He started saying things to belittle me, like I was acting like a little girl; threatening to be with other women who were ready. Then one night at his mom's house I just didn't fight him anymore. He said those magic trick words every playa says to the virgin girl, "If you love me then you will do it." Oh what a dummy I was. I actually fell for the okie doke on that one. It was a terrible experience, by the way. I remember crying during, afterwards, and days to come. There was no one I trusted enough to talk to except my best friend at the time, Sister. She was my first friend when I moved from Memphis to New Jersey. We were both in teller training together at New Jersey National Bank. Her father was a pastor. She had two sons, tons of brothers and sisters, and a baby daddy in Newark or East Orange, New Jersey. Can't remember which one, but I would drive her up there to let the boys spend time with their father. Boy did they not get along. I am talking about her and her baby daddy. All they did was fuss and fight, and about stupid stuff to. I used to be like, man I don't want NO KIDS now. Anyway, she was crazy about this guy who went to Saints of God Holy Temple, so we would always hang out at the guy's house on Brewers Avenue with a crew and his brothers. He and his brothers and one sister all lived in this house together, and they were a riot. The guy had a brother who could sing his butt off named Trey. Trey and I became something. To this day I don't know what we were because it was strictly platonic, but I loved his singing. Plus, it seems I was the only one without a boyfriend, so that is what I made Trey. I would buy him gifts, talk to him on the phone, and support him whenever he had a singing engagement. There was a joke going on behind my back because everyone, but me knew that Trey did not like girls, if you know what I'm saying. Finally, it came out because they told me, and busted out laughing me to scorn at my reaction. I mean I had never met anyone like this before, so I was so shocked and embarrassed. Not because Trey was gay, but because now my front was busted trying to pretend to have a boyfriend for show. Everyone thought I was so country, since I grew up in Memphis, Tennessee then moved up to Trenton, New Jersey. They called me their Memphis Belle, which is actually a cruise boat, so I did not like the name. You know, they still call me the Memphis Belle (laughing) to this day. Even though I did not like the nick name, I was a good sport about it, and just laughed it off when anyone would call me that. I remember thinking, these people are nothing like us back home, but then again I guess they were a little similar. They would shout and praise God in church, sing under the anointing, and do all kinds of sinful and lustful things at the same time. I was like, now how is God letting them get away with all this here. They got a kick out of me being so naïve. Just like back home in Memphis, I was thought of as Ms. Sweet, little, perfect patty scared of doing anything wrong or getting into trouble.

Well, in that relation with Trey, he was the problem because Trey was probably using me as a cover, but it really wasn't working. We used to frequently attend revivals, and musicals at Light of the Son Holy Temple. Turns out that Trey's whole family just about went there. He had this one cousin who seemed so mean, and his name was Lance. They would all hang out in the church parking lot clowning people.

Oh, I hated it, but I tried to stay quiet so they would not clown me. They were all a part of this community choir called The Unlimited Voice of Trenton, so after a while I ended up joining, traveling, and singing with them to. Lance liked me, but I just thought he was so mean. He always had a serious look on his face, and his voice was so commanding and strong. Seemed like lots of folks looked up to Lance, and he kept Trey and the rest of his cousins in check. In other words, Lance did not play. Found out he was also a preacher. I remember Lance would send a message to me when we all would go out to eat at a restaurant after singing at a musical. He would have the waitress tell me he was paying for my tab and sometimes my friend's to. Wow, I had never had a guy since Edmond to show me love and care like that. He had me blushing, and wondering what should I do. Long story short, he asked me to be his girl, and we started dating. I mean he made sure I was treated well everywhere we went, and he showed me off to his family and friends. I was nervous when it came time to meet his family because he had a mom, dad, sisters, and brothers just like Edmond. I feared they would not like me, or at least his mom would not like me. But I was wrong. To my surprise, I was a hit with them. Next thing I know, Lance was proposing to me in front of everyone at a Gospel concert. It happened during a celebration of the choirs musicians, then called the Preachers Boys Band, which Lance was a part of and helped start. How could I say no? I mean Lance was so nice, and now he had become my best friend in the whole world. At this point in my life, since I had never really felt loved or wanted by anyone other than my Aunt Bobbie and my Grandmother who we called Mama, I did not even know much about love. There are different types of love, and being in love was different than agape love. My family tried to beg and plead with me not to marry this guy, but I was afraid not to. After all, look at how nice Lance had been to me. I mean he went out of his way to love me, and care for me. Plus, this may have been my only shot at happiness, and getting my dream of marriage. Who else will want me? Let me tell you those are the wrong reasons to get married. Plus, we got pregnant right after the engagement, so what did I look like being a minister, supposed to be saved, and pregnant out of wedlock? I figured that we can just make it work, but the odds were against us. I mean, he had no money, no real job, no care, no crib. He had to move in with me. You know my grandmother used to say, "Pookie, how you start out is how you will end up." Boy was she right. I learned from this marriage not only is how you start how you will end up, but also things can only get worse than when you start out, so you better start out pretty high on the scale of things.

Now, in this relationship I was the problem just like many of you reading this are. You are in a miserable marriage or relationship right now. Yet, you are filled with too much pride to admit you messed up or are messing up. I got married number one because it was my childhood dream. Number two, I was pregnant. Number three, I did not want to let anyone down. None of these are reasons to get married. Not one reason was because of being in love. Why are you married? Why are you even with the person you are with? If God, love, and a God purpose are not your top three reasons, then you are the root problem to your relationship issues. You should marry for love and purpose and because God gave you permission, not out of fear or obligation. I know that now, so my next marriage will be for all the right reasons.

I Choose To Forgive

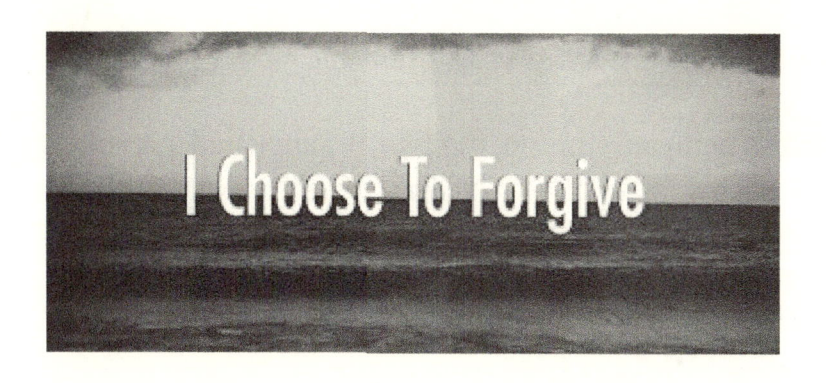

"But when that which is perfect is come, then that which is in part shall be done away. When I was a child, I spake as a child, I understood as a child, I thought as a child: but when I became a man, I put away childish things." **Corinthians 13:10-11.**

The Preacher's Kid

Oh, let me break it down for you. Being with a Preacher's Kid, aka PK is quite interesting. See, they can go many different ways. They can either be straight deceivers doing everything under the sun behind their parent's backs, or they can be raised up the right way and truly saved and sanctified. They can also be raised in so much toxicity that they can be self righteous or mean. I would say that the young man I met evolved from being a sinning thug to a sanctified preacher, but in the end became a tough cookie; to put it nicely. Let's call him Lance. Lance and I were so not compatible in many areas. I mean he was not a real go getter. His work ethic, well let's just say he had no real work ethic. He believed in having faith in God, some pie in the sky scheme, or that a miracle of money will fall out of nowhere syndrome. How I was raised is that if you do not work for everything you want, then it just ain't gonna happen. Our whole marriage just went from bad to worse. It was like a battle every day; a competition or fight to see how he could hold me back or keep me down because he was not accomplishing his dreams. At least this is the way I felt. My worse fear was that he did not want me to succeed. It seemed everything I tried to do he would shoot it down. Over the course of time, our relationship got so toxic. He became so controlling of my every move driving me everywhere, keeping our son and me away from my family, controlling everything I did; even the clothes I wore. He made me believe he was the only one in the whole world who loved or wanted me, and called me dumb basically brainwashing me into believing that if I ever left him that either he would kill himself or something bad would happen to me. Because nobody wanted me anyway, and I would just die old and alone. I remember the day he left. We did not have much of a marriage because we were living basically like roommates the last 3 years. Because I had to be the only one going out to work every day, cooking, cleaning, figuring out the bills, doing the homework with our son, and taking our son to his sports and auditions, over the years I was just exhausted. This is why I hated sex. I at least wanted to not have to do all the work in this area, but needless to say this was not the case even in this area. When you are a woman and the main one bringing the home bacon, frying it up, cleaning, caring for the children with whatever they need or having going on, working full time, trying to start a business, trying to go back to school, the last thing you want to do is all the work in the bedroom. About a month after our son was born I wanted out of the marriage, but after talking with a family member about it they said to me, "You made your bed, so now you have got to lay in it." I was like dang, but doesn't everybody make mistakes? What a blow to my heart, so I fought for the marriage from 1992-2006. I felt I was stuck in a marriage that I just had to make the best out of because I could NEVER get out of it. But then February 15, 2006 came, one day after our fifteenth wedding anniversary. He had relocated me and our son to North Carolina supposedly to replant our church, and have a complete fresh start. Then he gets me to agree with yet another bright idea; a plan for him o go back to New Jersey for a few weeks. He was only supposed to be gone for thirty days to tie up some loose ends, so he said. Thirty days because five months. He abandoned our marriage, in my heart. If your spouse leaves on business, but what is supposed to be a month long stay turns into a five month stay then something is seriously wrong; especially if there is no proper communication. Something is really wrong when they refuse to see you. Where they do that at? I believe it was like November of that year when he finally told me he wanted to come home. You will have to learn in another book what happened in those nine months, but what I can tell you is that a whole lot can happen in nine months of being apart from your spouse. Yes, by this time I got tangled up into an unimaginable temptation and web. In the end I believe Lance and I both learned from all our mistakes. Still sometimes, I am in awe at the beautiful and anointed couple we were working in ministry and pastored a church together, prophetic, anointed, and appointed; yet we allowed Satan to kill, steal, and destroy our marriage. We knew God, and the word of God. We were used by God to pray for many, cast out demons, and healed many that were sick with medical documentations and testimonies. Yet, we were robbed because we did not get proper counseling and tools we needed to help keep our marriage healed and together. There are many suffering in the body of Christ ready to give up on your marriage, and I encourage you to go back to God. Stop! Do not make any final decisions without God. *"Jesus said unto him, IF thou canst believe, **all things are possible** to him that believeth. And Jesus looking upon them saith, With men it is impossible, but not with God: for with God **all things are possible."*** **Mark 9:23; 10:27**

By this time in my life I was so full of despair, heartbreak, and grief I just did not trust anybody and had an "I don't care" attitude to life. Door opened wide open for Satan to walk back in my life, but worse this time. *And then I* met Trey.

I therefore, the prisoner of the Lord, beseech you that ye walk worthy of the vocation wherewith ye are called, with all lowliness and meekness, and longsuffering, forbearing one another in love: Endeavoring to keep the unity of the Spirit in the bond of peace. There is one body, and one Spirit, even as ye are called in one hope of your calling; One Lord, one faith, one baptism, on God and Father of all, who is above all, and through all, and in you all. But unto every one of us is given grace according to the measure of the gift of Christ. And be renewed in the spirit of your mind; and that ye put on the new man, which after God is created in righteousness and true holiness. Be ye angry, and sin not: let not the sun go down upon your wrath: neither give place to the devil"
Ephesians 4:1-7, 23-24, 26

Keeping it Real

This is the let's keep it fa real, for real section. I really do not have time to worry about what people will say about the things I share. I spent to much of my life thinking that every person in church were doing the right things. Do you know I sat up in church most of my life thinking that since the more seasoned saints were getting on me that they were so sinless that I had to make sure I had no sin in my life??? Where they do that at? I mean no matter how wonderful a person looks or smells he or she still have a stinky, sinful nature that will be a part of us all for the rest of our lives. Took me a long while to figure this thing out. There is no way any of us can suppress and stop every single thought or desire that tries us. The bible teaches us, ***"As it is written, There is none righteous, no, not one: For all have sinned, and come short of the glory of God; Being justified freely by his (God's) grace through the redemption that is in Christ Jesus: But to him (you) that worketh not, but believeth on him (Jesus) that justifieth the ungodly, his (your) faith is counted for righteousness. Even as David also describeth the blessedness of the man, unto whom God imputeth righteousness without works, Saying, Blessed are they whose iniquities are forgiven, and whose sins are covered.***

Blessed is the man to whom the Lord will not impute sin. For if they which are of the law be heirs, faith is made void, and the promise made of none effect: Therefore (you) being justified by faith, we (you) have peace with God through our Lord Jesus Christ: By whom also we have access by faith into this grace wherein we stand, and rejoice in the hope of the glory of God. And not only so, but we glory in tribulations (jacked up situations) also: knowing that tribulation worketh patience; And patience experience; and experience, hope: And hope maketh not ashamed: because the love of God is shed abroad in our hearts by the Holy Ghost which is given unto us. But God commendeth his love towards us, in that, while we were yet sinners (and sinning), Christ died for us. For if, when we were enemies, we were reconciled to God by the death of his Son (Jesus), much more, being reconciled, we shall be saved by his life. Wherefore, as by one man sin entered into the world

(Adam), and death by sin; and so death passed upon all men, for that all have sinned. (Romans 3:10, 23, 24; 4: 5:8, 13; 5:1-5, 8, 10, 12).

Do you get it yet? After reading all that good news right there do you get it? Is the smoke clearing? Let me break it down for you. **WE DO NOT SAVE OURSELVES OR MAKE OURSELVES RIGHTEOUS.** It is virtually impossible for you to do anything to make yourself righteous. There is only one thing you can do to make yourself the righteousness of God. Don't miss this now. It is simple. Believe in everything about Jesus, and receive him as your savior. That's it. After that, what you do is focus on serving him then God will do the rest. I am a living witness that when you stop hanging around, thinking about, talking about, meditating on all the wrong YOU think that you are then you give God the chance to show you the good you through his eyes. Do you know how beautiful and blessed you are? You have the right, and full access to the kingdom of God, and all the benefits that come along with that. But I have learned that when you keep dwelling on the bad you will never see the good. When you keep hanging around with the wrong then you will never get with the right. When you keep messing around with broke then you will never experience abundance. **It is a matter of choice. Do you choose life or death? Do you choose failure or favor?** If you are serious about wanting a fresh start, and wanting a better life then I encourage you to do what I did. Make a commitment to turn your back on anything and anyone who cannot help you to be the child of God that God desires us to be. It does not have to be forever, but it has to be for a season. All these years you have been in the mess you are in give God a year, 9 months, 6 months of you doing everything in your power to put God first over everything every single day; First Salvation, the

Sanctification, and then being baptized with the Holy Ghost. Not necessarily in that order. It works!

"For I am not ashamed of the gospel of Christ: for it is the power of God unto salvation to everyone that believeth; to the Jew first, and also to the Greek." **Romans 1:16**

The "I Don't Care" Attitude

Getting back to my craziness when I had the **"I don't care attitude."** There is a period of time in your life that you can become so blind, confused, and lost. This especially happens after you have suffered from being the victim of abuse or a romantic break up. I went through this period, and was blind to it while I was going through it. I mean, I was blind to what the enemy was trying working in my life. Just like some of you reading this book, I just went with the flow and let life happen. On top of all of the grief and guilt Satan really works on trying to make you believe you are alone and there is no one to trust. This was a very painful experience for me. Because I was the Evangelist, the Pastor, the Teacher, the Woman of God, who could I trust? Who could I go to? I mean, people did look to me for answers, prayer, and support? So many people, especially my peers, depended on me so much until there was no way I could let them see me like this. I found myself vulnerable and feeling threatened that all the people I have preached and ministered the word of God to will now see me in a poor and miserable state. The first thing I tried to do was go through my phone list of all the pastors and bishops Lance and I had been connected to. Not one even tried to offer counseling or hope to our situation. As a matter of fact some even talked to me sexually saying things like, "As beautiful as you are, if you were mine I would …" Imagine that. You go to the ones who are suppose to be church leaders, and realize they are just as carnal and perhaps even more lost than you. A few even talked trash about Lance. It was so bad that I had to do a 3 way call with Lance to let him secretly here one of his close friends talk to me. It hurt us both terribly. The devil used this as a foot hole to come at me with all manner of sexual thoughts and images which ultimately because desires. Before this point, I had never thought about another man other than Lance, or sexual stuff. **Galatians 5:9** teaches us that *"A little leaven leaveneth the whole lump."* But God has taught me a very needed lesson on church leaders from my experience. Psalm 146:3 says "Put not your trust in princes, nor in the son of man, in whom there is no help." What this means is even the most powerful or greatest leader cannot help you. The most influential and prominent leader you cannot fully trust. Yes, we are to be held to a higher standard of integrity, but unless a person has accountability for that how can they possess Godly integrity? And for those who do have a covering or someone who is mentoring them, but have not been planted in the sanctification through the word of God then they are blind to. Matthew 15:14 Jesus teaches the disciples, "Let them alone: they be blind leaders of the blind. And if they blind lead the blind, both shall fall into the ditch." Now don't get me wrong, a sanctified leader will mentor sanctification and for us all to be lead by the Holy Spirit. That no matter who we are, or what title or office we hold in the body of Christ, we are still human and need to make sure we have daily bread with God; acknowledging Him in all our ways so He may direct our paths" **Proverbs 3:6**. Until a person, even a church leader has fully adopted sanctification as his or her way of life; they will continue to fall into a sinful nature. They can only let you down if you trust in them more than you trust God. No matter what the title or position a person has they are still human, and subject to the same temptations we are every day. This is why God has instructed me that it is so very important for our own salvation to not put people on a pedestal, or expect more out of them than they are capable of giving. You must forgive them, pray for them, and give them over to God. There are a lot of good, bible believing, gospel of Jesus Christ teaching, sanctified pastors out here. Keep searching until you find one that you can respect enough to sit under to be planted and prosper in the things of God. If you don't, God will hold you accountable for not working out your soul salvation because only you are in charge of that. Show God that He is the only God in your life, and no person will be more important than obeying Him. We don't think about being idolaters and serving other little gods, but if we are not careful we can also make people a God when we are more concerned about what they do and who they are.

Okay, back to the break up with Lance and I. It all started with us having a troubled marriage, and us never fixing that. Then, separating and being apart from one another for a long period of time. Then, we were leaning on man instead of God for all our answers.

After a preacher was inappropriate in conversation with me on the phone, I started getting involved in this online chat that I had stumbled across. Then I started opening pop ups on my computer from porn sites, then I started watching porn, then I started buying sex toys, then I started burning with sexual desires to be with a man; any man. You see how slick Satan will work on you? It starts with just one conversation, one TV show, one song, one drink, one party to give the enemy a foot hole into our lives to draw us away with our natural lusts away from God. Satan preys on the weak. Read **Joel the 3rd Chapter**. The prophet made reference about the children of God being put into captivity, and how God will allow them to go through many things. How even through all of what they go through, the children of God must still get up their weapons and fight back. **Joel 3:10** says, "Let the weak say, I am strong." Just like the children of Israel, we have to also put up our weapons and fight back when the enemy works in our mind and our emotions to get us to obey his commands instead of what God commands us to do. 2 Corinthians 10:4-6 teaches us what our weapons are not and how to fight. "For the weapons of our warfare are not carnal, but mighty through God to the pulling down of strong holds;

Casting down imaginations, and every high thing that exalteth itself against the knowledge of God, and bringing into captivity every thought to the obedience of Christ; And having in a readiness to revenge all disobedience, when your obedience is fulfilled. So you see no matter what you do or somebody else do, you still must go back to God and search our your own heart in prayer to make sure that you are putting all of your trust in God; that all of your actions and decisions are based upon following God through His word, and not any man.

You reading this right now may be going through some of these same things I went through, or knows of someone who is. What does it matter if you are a church leader or not? What does it matter if you went to a church leader and they let you down? We are all still human, born in sin, and shaped in iniquity. But glory be to God that Jesus came, and we no longer have to live under the law of sin because **Romans 8:1**

and 5:2 teaches us; "There is therefore now no condemnation to them which are in Christ Jesus, who walk not after the flesh, but after the Spirit. By who also we have access by faith into his grace wherein we stand, and rejoice in hope of the glory of God."

I remember while I was pregnant with my second child, I went and drew up a living will; Ended up trying to decide if it would be my last will and testament. Yes, I wanted to die. I mean, how was I gonna now go from being this perfect patty, grand woman of God, loved, and respected by all to this nobody of a person living in guilty shame, pregnant with one man's child while I was not even sure about if I wanted to stay married to the other one? How was I gonna face myself, let alone others for letting God down; letting everyone down. I felt that I had the world on my shoulders. I just wanted to go to sleep, and not wake up again. But there were 2 things that kept me going; my teenage son, and my beautiful son I was carrying. See, even though you may be having thoughts of suicide, guilt, hurt, shame, helplessness God still has the power to shake your world and remove every demonic hindrance that has come to destroy you. God is the destroyer of the destroyer. I was so weak and burden, I could hardly get out of bed or walk. I lost so much weight during my pregnancy. As a matter of fact, I almost lost my baby 4 times. The last time it happened was during the month of April. My baby was not due until June, but here I had made myself so sick that I went into full labor. They had to stop the labor, and put me on bed rest. I remember, that day I cared about the life I was carrying enough to finally care about myself again. All those times you just do not even care about yourself, God is right there just waiting for you to see Him in your situation. So much good can come out of what you are going through. I am not going to lie to you, and say it is easy because it is not easy. It is not easy to see good in a bad situation. It is not easy to see God through all the hell Satan is putting you through. Just know that God has allowed you to go through this painful situation, and since He promised never to leave or forsake us, then surely God will make sure **YOU WILL SURVIVE**. You will survive just like I have to learn some life lessons that you will one day teach others.

****

STOP! Go to YouTube or where ever you can find the song, "The Battle is Not Yours" by Yolanda Adams. I want you to listen to this particular word especially if you are hurting. The words say no matter what you are going through God wants to use you. The battle is the Lord's. Hold your head up high, don't you cry. Sit someone by yourself, close your eyes; get on your knees if you have to. Get in a position that says to God I surrender my will to you. Give it all to God, in the mighty name of Jesus. And for all those who want to gossip and judge the content of this book, go burn it and leave it alone because this book is not for you. Everyone else, see you in the next section after you listen to the song.

Romans 6:23

For the wages of sin is death; but the gift of God is eternal life through Jesus Christ our Lord.
Romans 6:23

The Trap House Thug

Thugging and gangsta style living is a way of life for so many in the so called "hood." I remember when I was growing up, the word hood was just short for neighborhood. Now, it has taken on other meanings. Thugs and gangstas live a whole nother life outside of what you and I might call normal society. They don't trust anyone outside their circle. They look for hook ups instead of shopping in stores and work instead of a regular job. Even though they make out good with the hook ups and making all that fast money, there is a price to pay for many when the wrong move is made.

God bless all the sista's and brotha's that make it out of that lifestyle into a more peaceful and prosperous life.

Well I met a guy who was a straight up thug. See I believe a thug has little to nothing, and is all talk; a great manipulator. But when it comes down to taking care of responsibilities, some just do not measure up. Like the guy I met. Let's call him Trey. When I met Trey I had been introduced to a lot of sinful ways that I had never known before moving to N.C. You name it; I saw it or heard it. What I know now is that everything that you see and hear begins to control and shape who you are and what you do. In fact, it controls the kind of company you keep, and desires you have. Needless to say, the reason my estranged husband could not come back after being gone for five months was because I had wrestled with whether or not he truly loved me, whether or not a woman he said he befriended he was cheating on me with, whether this woman was the reason why he told me it wasn't a good time for me to see him, why did I marry him in the first place, was I truly in love with him, every single negative thing I felt I had endured from him in our marriage. I got to the point of convincing myself that my marriage was over, and that with or without a letter of divorce I was moving on. I mean don't people just move on? Who cares about all the particulars when you are angry and hurt and just want relief?

Well, I found out I was pregnant November 16, 2006. Pregnant! After all the years I had cried to have a baby, yes, pregnant. I went to the doctor for a bad stomach ache, and the exact words from the staff were, "Boy do you have a stomach ache." The enemy worked on scaring me into thinking God was punishing me, and that I was facing death as my punishment. See, this is why it is important for you to go to the doctor to get checked out instead of sitting there being stressed out assuming you are terminally ill.

I was thinking maybe I had a deadly disease or something, but no. This doctor actually fixed his mouth to inform me that after being told for fourteen years by my doctors up north that I had issues getting pregnant, my chance had finally come to have a baby. It had been fourteen years since my first child. Needless to say, I had almost given up hope of ever having any more babies. Let me tell you, I was in total shock, surprise, and upset all at the same time. Really, I just about had a breakdown right in the doctor's office. It was a total meltdown to the point that I was sitting in the floor crying and babbling that it's a lie –not true after all these years. And with this guy lord? Not this guy Jesus! Why! "Why Lord, why," I cried. People would sarcastically say, well it's because $a + b = c$, but I was just dumbfounded. I was like, now is not the time to be playing. After picking myself up off the floor, and putting myself back together in one piece, I ended up taking home an ultrasound picture of the baby's heartbeat, and drove from Asheboro to Randleman to sulk. Afterwards, the baby's father and I tried to make it work, but this was a doomed relationship from the start. I didn't want this guy for no relationship no how. He was not even saved. See, and what I did not know that this guy was a complete fraud, pathological liar, and thug. He was a petty drug dealer plus everything I had no experience of knowing how to deal with, so I was not even shocked when I found out all the house parties or get togethers he took me to, were actually being held in a trap house.

There was drug dealing, and prostitution going on right under my nose which I was so oblivious to. But God opened my eyes. There is a saying that you can't even see the forest for the trees. Well, I was so fascinated with partying and being grown, as we call it, that I was not aware of my surroundings. I think they all laughed at me being so gullible. Now, I found myself pregnant.

We were not even together when I found out I was pregnant. Even though I was a backslider at this point and far away from trying to live saved, God still had his hands on me. Yes, it is true. Once saved always saved, but honey let me tell you, this old world can entice you to experience some things that will have you thinking that God will stop loving you. But God never stops loving us. God spoke to the prophet in Jeremiah 31:3 saying, " The Lord hath appeared of old unto me, saying, Yea, I have loved thee with an everlasting love: therefore with loving kindness have I drawn thee." All you have to do is open us your heart. Read the **Jeremiah 3**, but pay attention to what God speaks in **verses 14 and 15**. "Turn, O backsliding children, saith the Lord; for I am married unto you….And I will give you pastors according to mine heart, which shall feed you with knowledge and understanding."

STOP! I want you to take a moment here and listen to the song, "Open My Heart" by Yolanda Adams. The song says show me how to do things your way. Don't let me make the same mistakes over and over again. Meditate on it, and cry out to God when you listen to it.

A Faith Confession

"What shall we say then? Shall we continue in sin, that grace may abound? God forbid. How shall we, that are dead to sin, live any longer therein? Know ye not, that so many of us as were baptized into Jesus Christ were baptized into his death? Therefore we are buried with him by baptism into death: that like as Christ was raised up from the dead by the glory of the Father, even so we also should walk in newness of life. For if we have been planted together in the likeness of his death, we shall be also in the likeness of his resurrection: Knowing this, that our old man is crucified with him, that the body of sin might be destroyed, that henceforth we should not serve sin. For he that is dead is freed from sin. Let not sin therefore reign in your mortal body, that ye should obey it in the lusts thereof. Neither yield ye your members as instruments of unrighteousness unto sin: but yield yourselves unto God, as those that are alive from the dead, and your members as instruments of righteousness unto God. For sin shall not have dominion over you: for ye are not under the law, but under grace. What then? Shall we sin, because we are not under the law, but under grace? God forbid. But God be thanked, that ye were servants of sin, but ye have obeyed from the heart that form of doctrine which was delivered you. Being then made free from sin, ye became the servants of righteousness." *Romans 6:1-7, 12-15*

Turning to God

"Turn, O backsliding children, saith the Lord: for I am married unto you" **Jeremiah 3:14**

See, this is the part that I wanted you to get through to. For all of you who have ever gone through any craziness choosing the wrong people and making unwise decisions this next part is for you. Maybe your situation is the same or worse than mine was. The point is that we ALL go through something. **It is up to you whether you allow that something to break you down or make you into a better person.**

After everything I had gone through God began to turn things around for me; making everything come full circle. Of course God can only do this when we want Him to, and I truly cried out to God and wanted Him to be lord over my life again. What I started learning, is that God truly never leaves you, and He will always show you the way, the truth, and the light; God is truly married to the backslider. The enemy tricking me in my heart, and my mind into thinking that I was better off dead; that I was a mistake and mess up was all giant lies. Listen, your life is more valuable than you think. Look at the stuff Satan fought me with. Look at the stuff Satan is fighting you with right now. Why do you think Satan has fought you tooth and nail trying to stomp the life out of you? It is because you are a super powerful and enormous threat to Satan's kingdom. God created you in His image and with his creative power. Think about how your life will look when you tap into God's power in you, and how many souls are going to be saved and set free through the words of your testimony. Will you get into a place where you can tell it? The true gospel of Jesus Christ is that we cannot become the righteousness of God without the redemptive work Jesus did on the cross at Calvary. **Because God knows that we cannot get it right in our own selves, all he requires us to do is**

accept Jesus Christ, and become his living examples of His word through faith.

Getting back to the story, about two weeks before I found out I was pregnant by Trey; I had finally had enough of his shenanigans. I had found out his name wasn't his real name, his car wasn't his car, his home wasn't his home, his job… well let's just say that just like character portrayed on the sitcom Martin - he ain't got no job. Well, not a real one anyway, and still to this day he has no real job. See, you have got to pay attention to the red flags of a person having a criminal past. Always wearing a white t-shirt may be a sign. No proof of so much of a high school diploma may be a sign. Talking about he does lawn work or odd jobs is definitely a sign. Him staying up and out all night long, and sleeping in late each day is a definite red flag my sista. Watch the people he hangs with and how they living. If he does not have his own car, and lives with family these two are the first two signs to say this man is not for you or ready for marriage. I mean let's keep it real, if you are a true sanctified child of God, you do date with a purpose right? I mean is your purpose to just get a man for some fun or to get married? If you are sanctified then you don't want to go around shacking up all your life. Eventually, you do want to settle down and have a husband and family to serve God with.

Okay, so getting back to Trey; he was such a deceiving manipulator. I mean I must have had dumb written right across my forehead when he picked me out. Plus, he had been locked up, and was fresh out of jail right before I met him. The devil really knows how to do a number on you. This guy had me straight tripping and mystified ripping and running the streets all types of night with him. I was in what I call the "I Don't Care" state of mind or the "I Don't Care Syndrome." Let me tell you, and you probably already know. Having an "I don't care attitude," will cause you to do things and go places that you would never dare to in your right mind. It will get your jacked up. You can get tangled up in things that you find yourself feeling trapped in and wanting out of, but not knowing how to get out. You get caught up in snares so tight, and bazaar that you sit around and wonder how in the world did I get in this mess?!

On a different note, even in my sin, I kept singing in the choir, and going to church, and hearing or trying to hear the word of God. The devil made me feel so convicted. Lance and I tried to reconcile. He was there for me during my pregnancy, and each time I went into the hospital for almost losing the baby, or got sick he prayed for me. I loved Lance so much because he took the time to tell me he was sorry for leaving me alone for so long without a covering or protection. I told him I was sorry to, for not being strong enough to handle my thoughts and temptation and fears. We really tried to attempt reconciling, but for me I just could not. There was still so much animosity, and resentment, and hurt between us, so without proper professional help how could we get back together and with a baby by another man. Anger and verbal abuse was already in our marriage before all of that happening. Lance refused counseling as always from day one of our marriage troubles. Trey was pulling on me on this side, and Lance pulling on me on the other side; both making threats towards one another and then towards me. I decided that I would divorce Lance, and be a single mom. I decided that I needed to make God my father again, and leaned on God for forgiveness, and answers.

I want to encourage every married couple. God wants you to know that He honors your marriage no matter who YOU chose to marry. There is no right or wrong person. There are only easy or hard people to work on staying married to. You can fight, live in two separate households, be all emotional and angry, but please DO NOT GET A DIVORCE until you have done and tried everything possible to make sure it is not going to work. This includes you BOTH going to professional and spiritual counseling. Go outside of your church if necessary, but get the help and tools you need to attempt at having success in this here marriage. Marriage is so serious. It is not just something to do. It is a covenant with God and with the person you marry, and is supposed to stay until death. If **YOU** do not do your part to do all **YOU** can do, then this here marriage will become the same thing in your next marriage and the marriage after that if you do not take heed. At the very least you will get your own personal healing. With you being healed from deep emotional hurt, at least you can move on emotionally and mentally healthy for the next relationship. We have far too many people walking around damaged and toxic from brokenness. If it does not work out, then okay. If it does work out, then at least you have a wonderful testimony that you did everything possible, and remained married to help somebody else pull through.

Prayer of Salvation

Dear heavenly father, I am a sinner and I know I have done wrong. But I am asking you today to forgive me. Create in me a new heart, and renew the right spirit in me. I believe that Jesus died for my sins, and rose from the grave and is now seated on your right now heavenly father. I thank you heavenly father for sending Jesus Christ and for forgiving me of all my sins. Wash me as I study hear your word, and I shall be clean as snow. I thank you for saving me on this day,

_____

Write your spiritual birth date here

If you have prayed, and received salvation I want you to write to me via email at healingbrokenheartsministry@yahoo.com and I will send you a free gift to help you continue to enjoy your new life in Christ.

Getting a Relationship with God

"Therefore being justified by faith, we have peace with God through our Lord Jesus Christ: By whom also we have access by faith into his grace wherein we stand, and rejoice in hope of glory of God. And not only so, but we glory in tribulations also: knowing that tribulation worketh patience; And patience, experience; and experience, hope: And hope maketh not ashamed; because the love of God is shed abroad in our hearts by the Holy Ghost which is given unto us. For when we were yet without strength, in due time Christ died for the ungodly. For scarcely for a righteous man will one die: yet peradventure for a good man some would even dare to die. But God commendeth his love toward us, in that, while we were yet sinners, Christ died for us". **Romans 5:1-8**

I really wanted to get away from both Trey and Lance bad, because I had experienced so much hurt with them, and for one thing I just did not know how to forgive them truly, so I could get over it all. After having the baby, the devil beat me up so bad with condemnation that I would go to church hung over or drunk, and get drunk ever Sunday night trying to drown out my guilt and pain. From the time Lance left until I sought restoration with God was about 7 years. During these 7 years, I did any and everything I was big and bad enough to do. I partied hard and got drunk at least 5 days a week, cussed like a sailor, danced like a rock star, jammed to hip hop and gangsta rap songs, and had as much sex as possible. Yes, me; little perfect patty. You or someone you know is doing the same things. But hold on, there is victory after this.

The reason I wanted to be open and honest with you reading this book is because if someone had been open and honest with me, then maybe I would have found the knowledge, strength and faith in God that I needed instead of allowing life to take control of me; booting God out of the equation. See, we all need God. Without God we are nothing especially when we are born again, blood washed believers who have allowed the enemy to sift us as wheat. **_Luke 22:31-21_** *reads "And the Lord said, behold, Satan hath desired to have you, the he may sift you as wheat: But I have prayed for thee, that thy faith fail not: and when thou art converted, strengthen thy brethren."* By the time you read this book, your heart will be changed, and you will be on your way on a new path. **No more** will you be ashamed of your past or present. **No longer** will you submit to all the lies the Satan has planted in your head about you, your family, you're your future. **No ever** will you succumb to the deep emotional hurt that has held you crippled and captive for far too long. You will now rise up and walk out of your pain and be processed into your purpose! Remember, to share the goodness of the Lord, and intercede for others.

21 Days to Inner Healing

I want to take this time to share with you a very useful program, 21dayjourney.com, that helped me discover how to take control of my emotional health. I teach the class from time to time, and you can always register for the next class by emailing me at vfowler@healingbrokenheartsministry.org. While in the class, you will discover where all of your thoughts and perceptions about God and yourself have come from. You will also learn how to allow the holy spirit to help you take control over your emotions, so that you will have healthier and lasting relationships with family, friends, and your mate. It is a class that I love sharing and learning from over and over again. I look forward to you signing up for my next class. Go there now to the website and check out the introduction.

Remember Your Brothers and Sisters

I used to be so self-righteous because I had never did the things my friends did growing up. I missed all the hip hop era, and going to house parties. I was a virgin for a long time until right before my first marriage. I was the one all my peers looked up to for guidance and direction on living holy and saved. I used to think that oh no, if a preacher or a pastor did certain things, he or she should be taken down if he or she committed acts of sin willfully. I was so puffed up; so wrong. Don't laugh at me because you or someone you know is just like that right now, and you know it (laughing) But it really is not funny when you are hurting others. Just like me, you all need to stop all that. Love people for who they are, and not who they can become. That is how God loves and accepts us, and how God expects us to love and accept others. I mean God will judge all things when Jesus comes back. Leave all that judging to God, and just love.

Anyway, so when I turned to my sinful nature I could not stand myself; being filled with anger and disgust. I thought God had given up on me, so basically I gave up on God accepting me as his child. I thought that it wasn't for me; that because I was this big disappointment to people that because people turned their back on me that perhaps God had turned his back on me. Certainly, I thought, that God will never ever again in life use me again to be anointed to preach, sing, or teach anything in his church or to his people. Oh but, **Romans 11:29** teaches us that *"For the gifts and calling of god are without repentance."* Not only as humans are we capable of not repenting of the things we do, and still remain anointed to do God's ministry, **God does not repent or take back who he has anointed us to be.** If we decide we want to steal and preach then we will be an anointed preacher with a prison ministry, locked up still anointed by God. If we decide to be a dancer on a pole and sell our body for money and still sing on the choir, then we will just have to live with the guilt of being a strung out stripper, and still anointed by God. This is true whatever the case might be. This is a truth we all have to learn. We have to learn things can get better, and people can get better if we just let God tend to then, and we tend to God's word. We are to love, not judge, and strengthen those who are weak. We are to love ourselves, God and others.

When we see our brothers and sisters, and bishops and pastors, and singers and musicians, etc. weak; falling prey to temptation what do we do? What do you do? What have you done? Did you do as **Romans 15:1**, *"We then that are strong ought to bear the infirmities of the weak, and not to please ourselves"* Is this what you do, or do you send the person into isolation with the very sin and sinners they need to get away from? The bible says, *"For all have sinned, and come short of the glory of God,"* **Romans 3:23**. This is the reason why we all need to regroup, and rethink what we are doing. Many souls have been lost and driven out of the church because they have been treated like leapers, and pushed away as outsiders, rejected and not accepted. Oh, and the world will gladly take anyone the church is willing to push away. Did we forget how God forgives and loves us?

We all look like Jesus to God because Jesus stands over us and in front of us and has hidden our sins. God has declared it in his word, *"For ye are dead, and your life is hid with Christ in God,"* **Colossians 3:3**. Therefore I had to do what many of you will have to do who are reading this book right now. I had to face God, and get with God about my own situation; to drown out people and everything else hindering me. The more I praised God the more spiritual strength I got. The more I went to church, the more joy I got. The more I read the bible, the bolder against sin I got. The more I listened to gospel music the less I wanted to be angry. The more I sang the songs from Zion, the less I wanted to cuss folk out. The more I pressed my way to God the less I wanted to press my way to the club. The more I got into the presence of God, the less I wanted to be in the presence of sin. I begin to desire the presence of God more than the devices I had used to a temporary fix. But **it was not me who stopped me from all out sinning, and being angry; IT WAS GOD through His word**. The more I talked and prayed to God, the more I began to trust him; the more His word was made manifest in my life. The more I hungered and thirsted after God's righteousness, the more I wanted to be in the House of God. The more time I spent with God, the less time I wanted to spend with those ratchet friends who just liked to get wasted and party all the time. **God did it!** I began to see **<u>Psalm 37:4</u>** manifest in my life, *"Delight thyself* *in the Lord; and he shall give thee the desires of thine heart."* I began to practice **1 Corinthians 14:1**, *"Follow after charity (love), and desire spiritual gifts."* I went through praying to God about **Romans 7:21**, *"I find then a law, that, when I would do good, evil is present with me."* Sin feels real good and fun, but it keeps us away from God, and kept me in self-condemnation; believing the lie that God had forsaken me.

The problem with a lot of us, is that **we focus too hard and too long on what is wrong with us instead of what is right with God who is in us.** But then **2 Corinthians 11:12** began to be a practice in my life so that I had the strength to cut off all the men, and women, and temptations that would come after me; *"But what I do, that I will do, that I may cut off occasion from them which desire occasion."*

I gave no more occasion and opportunity for sin to control me. That sin; that ugly stuff is not the real us. I want encourage you. If you are living in despair or about to give up hope to look again to God this time. Give him daily time with you. **It won't even take some of you 6 months to wake up to a totally new life full of God's favor and abundance.** That is, if you are willing to put the work in. See it is impossible for us to stop allowing our sinful nature to control us when we do not even have the faith to believe that we are the righteousness of God no matter what. **We did nothing to become the righteousness of God, but it was the redemptive work of Jesus Christ on the Christ that made us all now daughters and sons of God and God's righteousness.** We belong to God, and need to gain faith and power over everything trying to trick us into believe there is no better life for us, and that we are hell bound. The only way we can go to hell is if we do not stop living under the curse of the law of sin. **Start living under the gift of grace through faith in Jesus Christ.** The old saints used to say when the church catches a fish God will clean it. Let yourself be caught by the word of God. Then the more you get caught up in the word of God, God himself will clean you and make you into someone you can be proud of. This book is only for those who want a new life hidden in Christ full of the grace, riches, and success that only is found through obedience to God by living by his holy word.

Remember, God is not mad at you but He is in love with you. There is nothing you can do to stop God from loving you. He hates our sin, but forever loves us. There are so many brothers and sisters waiting to hear your testimony. God wants to use you to set others free.

A New Beginning: Sexy Jay

When you have been betrayed by someone you love, the pain hits harder and deeper probably than anything you have ever experienced. It slams you down, and throws you into this zombie like state of going back in time to almost every hurting moment you can remember ever happening to you during your entire life. As a matter of fact, every time you are hurt by someone you love you grieve. Your grief cycle can take you back as far as hurts that you experienced when you were a baby or toddler. But, you must go through the complete grief cycle for every single time you are hurt in order to completely deal with and get over the pain; every single time you are deeply hurt just remember to keep telling yourself your state of mind is only temporary. Jesus died so that we would be saved and healed from every wound.

Hurt comes in various forms. There is the obvious hurt from experiences; like losing a loved one through death, or a breaking up with the one person you chose to fall in love with. Then, there is hurt you experience from losing a job, getting your car repossessed, having a miscarriage, or being foreclosed or evicted from your home. The list goes on and on. The hardest loss, as far as a relationship, I can remember ever grieving at this point in my life is that of losing the man I loved on purpose. He betrayed me in one of the worse ways possible.

Forgiveness **IS THE ONLY WAY TO HEAL.**

"I took you from the ends of the earth, from its farthest corners I called you. I said, You are my servant; I have chosen you and have not rejected you. So do not fear, for I am with you; do not be dismayed, for I am your God. I will strengthen you and help you; I will uphold you with my righteous right hand all who rage against you will surely be ashamed and disgraced; those who oppose you will be as nothing and perish." **Isaiah 41:9-11**

The Young Sexy Seducer

After your heart has been broken, after a bad breakup or divorce, you may experience a period of helplessness and depression. If you do not have a strong relationship with God, you may even find yourself sitting in bars drinking your life away, or hanging out with folks having you getting high or other reckless things. The two reckless things I can remember doing was drinking way too much, and falling in the sack with men. See, we all have different ways and different devices the enemy uses against us to keep us as far away from the will of God as possible. See, Satan hopes that we will end up dying in our sin and join him in hell. Oh, but thank God for all the praying grandmothers, and mothers, and pastors; whoever has prayed for us over the years. Stored up prayers even from those who have gone on to glory still keeps God's hands on us. That's why you can only get but so far with doing what you thing you are big and grown enough to do. Oh the blood of Jesus still works even when we are doing our thing. You ought to thank God for those who have prayed over your life. It is because of their prayers that we are still alive, not swallowed up by death, diseases like aids, or strung out somewhere.

Getting back to the story, I have always been a late bloomer. My woman's day did not happen until I was 15. In middle school I was still wearing pony tails and bobby socks. Even though Edmond was my secret church boyfriend, I did not have an official open boyfriend without worrying about my mom beating the brakes off of me. That was, until I moved to New Jersey. I was eighteen when I briefly dated that dude Paul the cheater and serial baby maker. Even until this day I am usually the last one to get a joke. But I'm good people though. I have a good sense of humor to, but heartbreak is no joking matter especially for an inexperienced young girl. The things I needed to get, and understand I got right on time; especially after my experience during my wilding out day. I am sure you have had some of those. Some religious people say they were miserable in sin, but I beg to differ. I had a ball enjoying my good times.

I was working at Air Expo. About one year after working there, I began to notice this young man. But I was unaware of how much younger than me he. I really did not ask any questions, you know just going through the flow; until it was way too late. I mean I had allowed all my hurt to come back and open yet another door in my life; vulnerable to love again. He was 10 years younger than me. 10 years! Age ain't nothing but a number? Now that's a lie. Age mixed with character is more than some stupid number. Young is fine, but being young and dumb is not OK.

I noticed him more after I had my baby. We noticed each other, as a matter of fact, but we went a very long time without ever saying a word to each other. We watch each other. We smiled at each other. At some point we both tried to be at the same place at the same time at work just so we could bump into one another and get a little closer. I remember where I sat it was a great spot to see him each time he would go up the escalator back to his floor. He worked on the floor right above me after I was promoted from customer service to the account security group. He would smile at me, and I would smile back; all without saying a word, but somehow we both started having this attraction or crush for each other. "Why was this guy so fine Lord," I would ask myself every time I saw him. Ever met a guy like that. You know the one you know is nothing but trouble. Mary J. Blige sings a song about it. From his hair, to his teeth, to his shoes omg I had done fell into lust with this man we will call Jay. It was my secret crush because how dare we even try to have a relationship working at the same job; Funny how life goes though. Sometimes you know the oven is hot, but you still cannot resist wanting to touch it. Oh, a little dab will do ya (laughing).

I have learned that you cannot help or control who you fall in love with when the feeling inside and attraction becomes something inside so strong. Let me correct that statement. It sounded good, but just not smart. OK. You cannot help or control who you fall in love with when you allow what you are feeling and the attraction you have for someone to become stronger than God's spirit in you, and override the voice of the Holy Spirit down in your belly trying to direct you.

O.K. so, it wasn't until a while later that I found out he was asking questions about me. I guess he was trying to scope me out, and find out all he could about me before approaching me. What a turn on, right? **Danger! Danger! Warning! Warning! Run girl! Run!** I ignored all of the alarms going off in my head about this guy. We had one mutual friend named Frankie who was getting to know me, and telling my secret crush everything he knew about me. This mutual friend, Frankie, and I worked in the account security group together. In hindsight, I believe it played me. He knew what this dude was all about. But you know what they say, birds of a feather flock together. Yeah, Frankie wasn't right either, but I won't go there. Anyway, a group of us from customer service were chosen out of so many who applied to be a part of the pilot group to test out this work segment. It was a success because the department still exists to this day with the company. Anyway, Frankie and I were a part of this click at work who hung out together. Boy was everyone off the chain in this bunch (laughing), but for the first time in my life I was having loads of fun with friendly and fun people. Well, I did have a lot of fun until ….. but I was so happy that finally had a group of hang out buddies in North Carolina. I finally had some good friends, so I thought. At least I was not sitting home alone anymore, I thought. What a foot hole I gave Satan in my life, AGAIN, hanging out with this bunch. Let's just call them The Hommies.

The Hommies were so funny and fun to be around. It was just what I thought I need to get me out of my slump of my second biggest breakup in less than a year with my baby daddy, Terry. I had suffered with depression while I was pregnant, and no matter what I did to try to keep to myself, go to church, and keep going on it just did not go away. Have you ever gone through something like that? You are probably going through it right now reading this book. Just know that you are not by yourself. Life happens, and through trial and error we eventually find our way through learning lessons. I was diagnosed with severe deep depression, and was actually taken out of work for what they called intense outpatient group therapy. I will talk about that at a later date. The enemy used all this against me to push me into falling for yet another Mr. Wrong.

See, my husband, Lance, had left me on what he called business; tying up loose ends. He had promised to come back home no longer than thirty days. But thirty days became sixty days, and sixty days became ninety days. Before I knew it, he had been gone for five long months. When I asked him to come home he refused. Now, he had left in February. After our son was out of school for the summer, I sent him up to New Jersey to spend time back home with family and his friends, but especially with Lance because he missed back home so much. Our son was struggling so hard with our break up, so this was the one thing I thought would make him so happy. See, our son hated living down south. Well, we were in Randleman, North Carolina which is a small little country town. At the time the biggest attraction was the Super Walmart and Hardees; oh, and the frogs chirping in our little pond lol. Our son loved Hardees because they do not have them back home up north. Anyway, at the end of the summer when it was time for our son to prepare to come back for school, I asked Lance again if we can see each other and spend some time together. Oh, by the way, this is all before meeting Terry and having the baby. When I asked Lance to either come home with our son or suggest that I come to New Jersey he said to me it wasn't a good time. It wasn't a good time? At that point, during one of our conversations, all hell broke loose, and I just could not deal with the situation anymore. I mean I had a melt down and lost it. I mean five months is a long time for a husband to stay away from his wife, then on top of that refused to even see me? What in the ham sammich did he mean now was not a good time. Oh this is where the cussing began. I felt abandoned, lied to, let down, unwanted, and betrayed. I started believing that he had brought me down from New Jersey to North Carolina to leave me on purpose. There was no shaking it because he gave me nothing, no actions, and no words to help me to believe otherwise. It was like all my demons from growing up, hurt that had happened in our marriage; everything was causing me to feel under emotional attack. It was all the usual painful emotions you feel right after suffering a loss or deep hurt; as if someone you loved deeply literally died. Anger and helplessness just took over. I know somebody understands what I mean because you are in the same place I was in just 11 years ago. But God…. "If we confess our sins, God is faithful and just to forgive us or sins, and to cleanse us from all unrighteousness" **1 John 1:9**. Thanks God for giving us the gift of his grace, mercy, and love. Without it I have no idea where we would be. That was the background before getting into Sexy Jay.

"He will wipe every tear from their eyes. There will be no more death or mourning or crying or pain, for the old order of things has passed away. But as for me, afflicted and in pain – may your salvation, God, protect me. The blessing of the Lord, it maketh rich, and addeth no sorry with it. For Godly sorrow worketh repentance to salvation not to be repented of: but the sorrow of the world worketh death. Their sorrows shall be multiplied that hasten after another god: their drink offerings of blood will I not offer, nor take up their names into my lips There hath no temptation taken you but such as is common to man: but God is faithful, who will not suffer you to be temped above that ye are able; but will with the temptation also make a way to escape, that ye may be able to bear it." **Revelation 21:4; Psalm 69:2; Proverbs 10:22; 2 Corinthians 7:10; Psalm 16:4; 1 Corinthians 10:13**

What's Love Gotsta Do With It?

I want to pause right here to speak to all you who are married and reading this book. I also want to speak to those of you who want to or are planning to get married. Marriage is not to be entered into lightly. As a matter of fact the moment a man and woman believe they should marry each other they both immediately should start taking classes, spending time with God in prayer and fasting about marriage, and getting good counseling. The one thing I truly believe was the downfall of the marriage Lance and I had was that he refused to allow us to get any type of counseling from anyone. Somehow in his mind he had taught himself to believe that because he is anointed, and a pastor, and an apostle that no one on earth had enough no how or wisdom above him to teach or counsel him on anything especially concerning marriage. I guess us being together, sticking it out in our relationship with things always seeming to work out,

Lance must have thought that things would blow over and work out. How can you solve marital problems when you actually need professional and/or spiritual help? How can you stop be abusive when you grew up in an abusive home? How can you stop being dishonest when you grew up and your own momma and daddy was dishonest? How can you stop cussing and fussing when that is all you heard in your home when you grew up? Well, I will tell you. You can't. Not without being born again and filled with the Holy Spirit. There is no way you can make your marriage better and stay together when you continuously have problems that neither one of you can solve alone. There is no way you can be a better you or your spouse can be a better them without God. Plus, what is the real reason WHY you both got together in the first place? Why do you want them and why do they want you? The truth of the matter is when you get together, or get married for the wrong reasons it never works out. NEVER!

When you keep having unresolved issues and hurt over and over again in your relationship; things never just work out by chance, or because you LOVE each other. When you know you have problems and do not seek help to solve your problems, I hate to break this down to you, but things will never work out. When you see the signs that this person is not right for you, but you marry them anyway things don't just work out. Well not without some miracle or act of God. **Marry right and your bond will stay tight. Marry wrong and you won't last for long.** This is one of my signature t-shirts that you can order. Send me an email and I will send it to you.

Do not marry anyone until you absolutely know that God has given you His approval, and until you and your mate have done all the research and work to gain tools for success in marriage. It aint' gonna work just because you love God or love them. Let me leave that right there for you to marinate on.

A lot of people think that just because you have money, material things, have good genes, or even a relationship with God that you are the best thing since sliced bread as a candidate for marriage. Lance and I thought that we would be married forever because of our relationship with God. We thought that because of our anointing, church leadership, and titles that we had what it took to make our marriage work. But we never considered all our baggage, hurts, and scars from our past. We never considered the parts of us that were imperfect, dysfunctional, and toxic. We were doomed from the beginning because of our ignorance in thinking we were above losing any attack or immune to being destroyed by the enemy.

Let me say this, first of all you must be with the person you want to marry for the **RIGHT** reasons; not just for love because love is not enough to sustain a relationship. I think Tina Turner had a revelation from heaven when she recorded the song, "What's Love Got To Do With It." The song goes on to say that love is just a secondhand emotion. Guess what? This is true. And don't get married because you are pregnant. Ouch! I know I just helped somebody right there. Just because you are blessed with a gift of a baby does not mean that the person is a match for a future. Of course you must have love in your relationship, but there are some key elements I believe all successful relationships must have to be happy, healthy, and lasting. Here is the list:

1. Chemistry   5. Loyalty

2. Purpose   6. Affection

3. Order   7. Sacrifice

4. God   8. Forgiveness

The number 7 is God's number of completion. With these 7 ingredients, your relationships can weather any storm, and last indefinitely. 8 is God's number of new beginnings. I say that with each challenge and struggle to repeat this check list to make sure your relationship is strong in all of these.

I say relationships because relationship building does not start when we marry, but it starts from birth. All our relationships take work, and will not work or last unless everyone involved in the relationship does the work to do their part to make it work. If it is hard for you to have or live by any of these qualities, then you will always have relationship issue especially when it comes to marriage. Also, you should not pass blame on your spouse, business partner, or any other person you are have a relationship with when you find that your relationship is not working; unless you can quantify the tangible proof that you, yourself, have consistently exemplified ALL of the qualities listed above, and without fail during the course of your relationship. As a matter of fact, if you want a divorce, and your spouse does not make sure you judge the situation based on what you have done to consistently establish and perform every one of these qualities of character. If there is infidelity, so what. If there is lying, so what. If there is financial mismanagement, so what. What matters is what part have **YOU** played in making **YOURSELF** blameless? If you have not conducted yourself with ALL of these qualities, then you can conclude that you have been a part of the problem. I have a big warning for you. **DO NOT END YOUR RELATIONSHIP until** you, yourself have demonstrated all of the 8 characteristics twenty-four hours a day, seven days a week for at least one year. During this time you and your spouse should be getting counseling. A good sign that your relationship has a chance is when your partner is able to agree with you to do counseling. I promise you that if you all do the work, you both can stay together in the power and love of God to produce a good, lasting, and successful relationship. Try this with all your relationships at home, at church, or in business/work. That's another book, so let me just leave this right here for you to meditate on, and remember it takes more than love.

RELATIONSHIP AND OUR HISTORY

We all desire a happy and healthy relationship, at least more than not. Accomplishing that is easier said than done in many cases. There are so many different factors that can cause such a traumatic impact on a relationship to cause it to go straight to the dump. Then there are world views and social media that constantly project images that if a couple have romance and sex they can succeed with just these two components. Many of us who are the product of the "Baby Boomer Generation," went through a whole lot of negative experiences growing up in the 60s, 70s and 80s. I truly believe the 80s and 90s really brought on the true essence of society failing family. Of course the 70s, 80s, and 90s have a big popular trend of events that may have seemed like great ideas at the time executed, but the results of family casualties are still evident today.

Take for instance the 70s with the fall of President Richard Nixon and the Watergate Scandal; there was a big spotlight shining on the credibility of our country and its political leaders. It was all played out in the media revealing wiretapping and an big cover up about the wrong doings of Nixon and those involved in the incident. CNN reported in a 2015 article 70 historic moments from the 1970s (http://www.cnn.com/2015/05/21/world/gallery/70-historic-moments-from-the-1970s/). It was quite an eventful decade with great music, women's rights activists, terrorism, horrific murders, Apollo 13 spacecraft explosion, the Vietnam War, the rise of gay rights, Walt Disney World opened with a $3.50 admission, first U.S. Presidential visit to China to start that relationship, one of the first pornographic films to get huge attention, Deep Throat, the hostage crises at the Summer Olympics in Munich, the Miami Dolphins were the first NFL team in history to win a championship and be undefeated, the epic movie ":The Godfather," the Sears Towers, now the Willis Tower, opened in Chicago and is still the second tallest building in the United States, Martial-arts legend, Bruce Lee dies, the Twin Tower was completed, now gone from the terrorist acts of September 11, 2001, we saw the scary movie ":The Exorcist," pocket calculators were invented, gas prices skyrocketed with fuel shortages, Hank Aaron breaks Babe Ruth's home run record, Beverly Johnson became the first African American model to appear on the cover of Vogue magazine in the United States, Mr. Cassius Clay, aka Muhammed Ali, wins back his titles he was stripped of from not going into the U.S. Army by defeating the undefeated George Forman, we saw the Steven Spielberg's first hit movie "Jaws," Arthur Ashe became the first African American to win Wimbledon, Saturday Night Live was born, in 1976 our country celebrated the bicentennial anniversary of the Declaration of Independence, don't forget the lady star cast of the television show, "Charlie's Angels," Barbara Walters became the first woman co—anchor on a major network evening newscast signing a $1 million annual contract becoming the highest paid journalist at that time, and great TV sitcoms. Oh, and what about the Village People. They had hit songs such as "Macho Man" and "Y.M.C.A." with a huge gay following; still being song today. Jimmy Carter becomes our 39th President, and the whole country was intrigued by the premier of the miniseries "Roots," enjoyed the epic sci-fi movie "Star Wars." Steve Jobs, Steve Wozniak formed Apple Computer Company, and introduced the Apple

II computer along with Bill Gates' Microsoft. Do you remember the scary two day New York City power outage? August 16, 1977 Elvis Presley died, and the next month The Atari 2600 video game was released. Reggie Jackson leads the Yankees to a World Series win, and we rocked to the disco music sounds of John Travolta starring in the film, "Saturday Night Fever." What about the news of the first test tube baby being born; and the horrific largest mass-suicide in history which happened at the compound of the People's Temple in Jonestown, Guyana? Don't forget that Sony introduced a toy everyone loved, the Walkman, the conviction of the most notorious serial killers of all time, Ted Bundy, and Mother Teresa won the Nobel Peace Prize.

The 1980s were just an eventful. John Lennon was assassinated, the Pac-Man video game was released and the Rubik's Cube was popular, CNN was born. There was an assassination attempt on the Pope and U.S. President Reagan, the first woman appointed to the U.S. Supreme Court, and of course the Royal Wedding was viewed by millions on T.V. The scary new plague called AIDS took over, and the PC was introduced by IBM. We enjoyed the movie E.T., Michael Jackson's "Thriller," many fights broke out over the popular Christmas gift Cabbage Patch Kids, we got our first American Woman in Space, Ghandi was killed, and PG-13 Movie Rating was created. We enjoyed the movie "Back to the Future," there was a large famine in Ethiopia, a hole in our Ozone layer was discovered, Rock Hudson dies of AIDS, and U.S. singers record a charity single, "We Are The World." Then there was the first PC Virus, the Oprah Winfrey Show, DNA first used, the Berlin Wall Falls, the World Wide Web was invented, (http://history1900s.about.com/od/timelines/tp/1980timeline.htm) and of course there was the crack epidemic born, and massive people being imprisoned because of drugs.

The 1990s was just as eventful, as we cheered as Nelson Mandela was freed, was in amazement as Magic Johnson announces he has HIV, disgusted by the arrest of serial killer Jeffrey Dahmer, were enraged by the beating of Rodney King and non-guilty verdict (http://history1900s.about.com/od/timelines/tp/1990timeline.htm). Music went from Disco, to Pop to Hip Hop. Seems like in the midst of all the world news, inventions, wonder music, war, and other media news our country forgot about our biggest foundational commodity; Family.

Open sex and a corruptible government took precedence in the 70s, the infamous drug crack cocaine, and mass imprisonment of those involved with it destroy families, and whole communities, then Hip Hop came up to express all the anger, frustrations, and tribulation from a reality stand point on what a lot of Americans have been blinded or oblivious. All of these things caused a big divide between church and government, our country's founding principals were compromised, black/white, rich/poor, privileged/underprivileged, minority/majority race issues were once again and still remain a big peace killer. We wonder how did we become so divided, full of disunities, little to no peace or trust, and dysfunction on lower levels such as in individual families, but I truly believe as this country has become divided and dysfunction this same spirit has crept into the most bonded and successful families.

Relationships are not what they use to be. There used to be a time when families and neighbors were loyal and looked out for one another. There used to be a time that we prayed in schools, and held strict punishments. There used to be a time where we used to put God first through prayer at political meetings, civic meetings, church meetings, and family meetings. Right or wrong, our country stood on its beliefs and decisions unified on one accord. Right or wrong family stood together on their beliefs, especially biblical beliefs, and remained unified. It seems like we have just allowed the world to turn, media to hypnotize us, and life to cripple us. We have gone from grandmothers being AARP age and seasoned to being young thirty year olds and almost no wisdom, morals, or common sense. But there is hope for our nation. There is hope for your children. There is hope for our marriages. There is hope for our schools and government. There is hope for the endangered species, Family.

God speaks to us all in 2 Chronicles 7:14, "If my people, which are called by my name, shall humble themselves, and pray, and seek my face, and turn from their wicked ways; then will I hear from heaven, and will forgive their sin, and will heal their land."

You may ask, what name does God call His people? God calls us the redeemed, His righteousness, His elect, His children, His chosen, and a royal priesthood. Apostle Peter teaches us, in 1 Peter 1:2-5, 7-10, 13-16 "Elect according to the foreknowledge of God the Father, through sanctification of the Spirit, unto obedience and sprinkling of the blood of Jesus Christ: Grace unto you, and peace, be multiplied. Blessed be the God and Father of our Lord Jesus Christ, which according to his abundant mercy hath begotten us again unto a lively hope by the resurrection of Jesus Christ from the dead, To an inheritance incorruptible, and undefiled, and that fadeth not away, reserved in heaven for you, Who are kept by the power of God through faith unto salvation ready to be revealed in the last time. That the trial of your faith, being much more precious than of gold that perisheth, though it be tried with fire, might be found unto praise and honour and glory at the appearing of Jesus Christ: Whom having not seen, ye love; in whom, though now ye see him not, yet believing, ye rejoice with joy unspeakable and full of glory: Receiving the end of your faith, even the salvation of your souls. Of which salvation the prophets have enquired and searched diligently, who prophesied of the grace that should come unto you: Wherefore gird up the loins of your mind, be sober, and hope to the end for the grace that is to be brought unto you at the revelation of Jesus Christ; As obedient children, not fashioning yourselves according to the former lusts in your ignorance: But as he which hath called you is holy, so be ye holy in all manner of conversation; Because it is written, Be ye holy; for I am holy."

I want you to take a moment to absorb all this scripture. It is the good news and gospel of Jesus Christ. See, God never intended for us to broken, poor, sick, divided, divorced, lost, fearful, depressed; God wants us all, every one of us, to prosper and be in good health as our souls prosper. God wants us all to have healthy and thriving relationships and successful families. The fact is that if our soul is not prospering then our health will not be good. And what makes our soul prospers is us feeding, and nurturing our spiritual man. See, we can gain and enjoy all sorts of things in this world, but loose our soul and create bad health situations for ourselves. How about we all try this together; let's incorporate building our spiritual man in our daily living? Don't you want to be sure that when you pray God will answer? Don't you want to be sure that when you have a need it will be supplied just at you speaking God's word? Don't you want to believe that when the doctor gives you a bad report that you can open your mouth and declare God's word, and that God has the final say? It is more than just speaking words; it is about believing what you say. It is about having faith enough to believe in God's word, that every time you speak to your situation that a little more of it is hacked away at so that eventually it will be gone away through the God's grace in the mighty name of Jesus? Well, the only way that can happen is by increasing your faith just a little more each day through hearing God's word (reading and the preacher), so that you will know what to speak, how to speak it with all authority and power that God our heavenly father has placed inside of you. We all have this power. We all have the right and privilege to tap into this power, but only through the word of God which *Romans 1:16 says, "is the power of God unto salvation (from anything) to everyone that believeth; to the Jew first, and also to the Greek (non-Jew)."* Trust me when I say you have that power. I know that you have it because I have it, and I know that I have it because I learned God's word, and speak God's word, and apply God's word to my own life and circumstances then I have watched and witness God work on my impossible cases with outcomes far more better and greater than I could have ever imagined.

When you start a new job or position with a company, most set you up on what is called a ninety day probation period. Whether it is from day one, or the day after you complete your training module, there is always a probationary period for a company to decide whether or not you are definitely a good fit, trainable for the new position, or if they have to cut their losses and terminate your employment. Think of the next phase in your life as your new position in God. Jesus Christ and the Holy Spirit will be the department manager and team supervisor. You have just accepted the position of being a Child of God. Now, when you first receive the offer for the position, you are notified that there are some things you must, without question comply with. Of course if you comply, then you will receive the full benefits package with special awards, privileges, and powers. During training you will receive all the tools you need to do the job. You will need to attend training class daily by reading the bible, going to your local bible study, and attending church services. The outline is other than the two days you will be going to your local church to attend bible study and church services, the other five days you will need to fast, pray, worship, and do self-study of the Word of God. This is so you can retain the gospel you receive each week in bible study and church services. Of course, you will need to pay attention, take good notes, and be an active participant because you will be test. Life will test you. Temptations will test you. Emotions will test you. Your past will test you. Your family and friends will test you. People you know and don't know will test you. But the good news is that your tests will always be open book because you can reference through the bible to find the answers to all your tests. And what is even better, the right answer is always there; usually there is more than one answer. When you feel yourself not sure of what the answer is, then you will be required to take a period of time to fast, pray, and study God's word until you are sure of God's voice and receive peace of mind.

The point is that our relationship with God is the primary and foundation source that all of our other relationships are built on. **When you find your earthly relationships not working out then take a good look to evaluate and improve your relationship with God.** Try it, and I promise you that this time next year all your relationships will be healthy and blessed.

SUCCUMBING TO SEDUCTION

Both Lance and Trey were so extremely angry and hateful towards me after I let them both know that I would no longer be trying to deal with them. All through my pregnancy I was affected so much to the point that I almost lost my child four times. I lost so much weight from stress and depression that my pregnancy start and ending weight was only a difference of seven pounds. Who goes through a pregnancy and only gains seven pounds? The doctors were telling me that the baby would be fine, but that I would suffer, and they were right. Anyway, I came through the pregnancy, and began making plans about how I was going to now be a divorced and single parent. It is hard enough losing one man you love, but two is even tougher; then add experiencing both of these losses at the same time. Plus, on top of losing the two men I loved and trusted, my oldest son now wanted to leave me to go back to New Jersey to be among his family and friends. That is three losses all at the same time; really four because of losing my home and support back home by being a stranger in a new state. Well, there are more losses. I lost my ministry, lost my friends, lost my job, and just about lost my mind. It was like experiencing multiple deaths all at the same time. The only way I could have made it through this period of my life was by the grace and mercy of God. I truly believe because I stayed connected to the church that my faith was always nourished, and my courage and strength renewed. God wants to do the same for you. I encourage you to keep on going to church, singing in the choir, serving in some capacity even when you are going through hard times.

Since I really am a one man kind of woman I never really tried to have a lot of male friends at this point. Jay ended up being my one and only go to person and confidant.

Jay is almost ten years younger than me, and by the looks of Trey being twelve years younger than me this made me look like a cougar, I guess. The thing is, I never pursued any man in my life because the man has always pursued me. I thought a cougar goes after the man, but I could be wrong. Anyway, Jay pursued me, and he was such eye candy so I wanted him to pursue me. I remember our very first encounter was the first and last night that I got so intoxicated at a club that it wiped out my memory.

The gang at work that I had attached myself to wanted to go out to this club downtown in Greensboro. It was being talked up that many from our job and the who's who of the city would be there. I remember wearing this sleeveless chocolate dress with cream striped down the front of the dress. My bra was my purse, and I had my keys on a chain that hung on my wrist so I was hands friend. This was Jay's birthday weekend, but I did not know it at the time. His birthday is April 5th, but I think this was like on April 3rd or something. Anyhoo, I remember seeing him in that club that night. He walked up behind me while I sat at a bar, and whispered in my ear, "Do you need anything? Are you okay? Well, if you need anything I will be around." It had been a long time since I even allowed a man to get that close to me enough to whisper in my ear. Jay made me feel like I was melting. That night though, I was thinking I do not have time for any man. I wanted to be engulfed in throwing a pity party for myself, and drowning in my misery.

What I am about to say, you may have gone through a similar experience, so I want to be transparent and share this with you so if you are still stuck there you can be encouraged that your life can change just like mine did. You can be healed today if you receive it.

Well, as you can imagine, I am sitting in this club. Let me set the scene. You walk into the club, but as you are approaching the building you can hear the music bumping and see the line of people waiting to get in. We had VIP access because we knew the people throwing the party, so we did not have to wait in line. The club has a bar when you first walk in on the lower level with seating at the bar and along the wall. There is even a small corner in the cut where a band is playing live music if you walk all the way to the back of the club at the end of the bar. Back off to the right of the club, when you first walk in the door there is a doorway leading up to the second and third floors of the club. On the second floor of the club there is a DJ booth, and nothing but a large dance floor. The disco lights are flashing. Where the large part of the dance floor is it is packed with people dancing and standing along the walls. If you walk through the crowd to the front of the building the front is all window where you can stare down to see the people on the street walking, car traffic, and the line of people waiting to get into the club. Now the band downstairs is playing nice R & B songs. On this floor they are playing rap and hip hop music. There is a sound barrier that you cannot hear anything or any music from either floor. Then there is the third floor. This is the floor that was set up with a bar and like a lounge area with leather sofas, but enough space to have dancing as well. This floor is crowded with people also, but it was in contrast to the second floor. People on the second floor wanted to dance and people on the third floor wanted to mostly stand around and drink as much alcohol as possible. The third floor is where I decided to sit and stay.

When my hanging partners first got to the club, all the ladies decided we would all get a martini special. This was nice, but I was not ready for what the devil had in store for me. While sitting there at the bar someone decided that after our martini that we all needed to drink a shot. A shot is a small little drink of liquor in a small shot glass, but the effects of it is huge. Not even finished with the first martini I still drank a shot. It was a shot of patron tequila. Oh, I learned that day what shots will do to you if you are not careful. So after we all chanted and throw the shot down our throats in one gulp I decided to stay seated at the bar while the rest of the ladies went back down to the second floor to dance. Seems like these girls were pros at drinking, guess they were breaking me in. As I as finishing the martini, I decided I wanted a second martini because it was not as strong as the shot. So I ordered another martini, and sat there enjoying the music that was being played on the third floor.

The music on this floor was music from like the 90s era mixed with current hip hop and R & B music. Keeping count, I was finishing now my third drink. All of a sudden someone comes up asks me what I was drinking, and offered to buy me another one. My first thought was no this is not my birthday or anything so I need to not have anymore. Plus, this was April and I had just had my first drink of liquor in December which did not give me enough experience drinking. I tried to say no to the drink offer, but the person insisted; told the bartender to put it on their tab and after the bartender gave me the drink they left. It was another shot of patron. Listen, I do not know how many times this happened, but it happened enough that I loss count after about five different people had walked up to me buying me shots of patron. It was a set up.

I remember spazzing out on a guy who tried to lure me into going to the bathroom with him. This is how women get molested and raped in clubs. God was definitely covering me because I don't care how much I knew not to go anywhere with a strange man, drinking can make some people not think straight. Have you ever been there? But what I do know is the law protects us from criminals who try to use a girl being drunk as permission to try to rape her. If this has ever happened to you, I want you to receive your healing and know that it is NOT your fault. Criminals know EXCACTLY what they are doing. Ask God to help you forgive yourself because guess what; God has already forgiven you for drinking those drinks. God wants you to receive his love, and start loving yourself more.

I remember my hanging partners coming to check on me a couple times, and Jay. But they just left me sitting there by myself drinking, and not watching what I was doing. Then again I was grown, so why should someone have to watch over me? Thank God that angels were watching over me. What I learned is that sometimes while you are drinking alcohol, you do not realize when you have had enough because you do not get very intoxicated necessarily while you are drinking. And the younger you and more inexperienced you are the more the affects of liquor can creep up on you. Later on, and after the fact is when it all hits you at one time. If you count at least 5 more people had offered me shots after I had already had two martini's and two shots of patron already. I started to feel sick.

The room was spinning, but I was sitting down. I felt like I was leaning to one side while someone was spinning me around in my seat, but I was sitting down not physically moving at all. I began to hold my head and close my eyes, which made the spinning worse, and could not get any relief. Also, I remember not being too friendly or nice to men who were coming up trying to talk to me. I felt so sick. Then I started thinking how in the world was I going to get home since I had driven myself. What a dilemma I was in. Have you been there? Then, I thought, well maybe one of my hanging buddies can drive me home. The thing is, you are supposed to have a non-drinking designated driver before you even leave home to go out. I wasn't thinking just like many of you reading this book. I thought I would just have one or two drinks then have a few hours for it to wear off, but this time I had drank mad drinks. To this day I don't even know if the nine drinks I counted were all that I had. Anyway, I had to figure out how I was going to get home or plan to ride home with someone else.

You reading this right now are probably reminiscing on the many ways of escape that God gave you when you were way out of your league, doing your thing, thinking you're grown. Oh, But God has God for your grace and mercy that brought me through. Through this book God is bringing you through to.

Back to the club scene, all of a sudden two of the ladies in my crew came up to me, Linda and Sheryl, and I could hear them say, "Niecy, give us your keys. Niecy give us your keys. We are not gonna let you drive." I appreciate them for being so experienced with drinking that they recognized that I could not drive myself. They probably saved my life. But then how was I going to get home. I figured since they were taking my keys that we would leave my car, and then I would ride home with one of them until I could sober up. But no. That is not how it went down. See when you sinking in sin, you cannot predict how low you will go. That is another subject for another time.

What happened next is that someone came up with the bright idea that Jay would drive me home. Actually, our mutual friend, Frank, suggested it after everybody else had decided that no one wanted to drive my car or take me home with them because they were all too drunk and wanted to be boo'd up, as they call it. How is it that we all come out together, but everyone decides to get boo'd up and leave someone hanging?

How convenient that my heart throb would get a chance to take me home. Then, like in some movies, snippets and moments in time is all I can remember from that night. I remember noticing that Jay was driving me home in my car. I remember starting at the bottom of the stairs where I lived, then standing at the door trying to figure out which key would open the door. I remember being inside my apartment in my bedroom and Jay undressing me because when he untied my dress from around my neck and undid my bra all my money and id fell out on the floor. I remember this because the room was still spinning, I had my heels still on, and I was trying to figure out how I would manage to pick up my stuff as I looked at it feeling like I was going to pass out. Then I remember lying in the bed and seeing Jay close my bedroom door. I remember this vividly because I do not like being in a pitch dark room, and I was screaming inside for him not to close me in the room in the dark, but nothing would come out my mouth. It was like gravity was tying me down to the bed, and making my lips too heavy to move or my voice to speak. Next, I remember that I was completely naked under the covers, and I had never slept completely naked before. I was freaking out about having a man in my home, and being so drunk that I cannot move. This was crazy! I kept thinking, "I am completely undressed with a man here." But all I could do is close my eyes and pass out.

The only other memory I have until this day is waking up the next morning seeing Jay naked in bed with me. I was so frightened that I backed all the way out of the bed onto the floor just gasping for air, with my jaw dropped, covering my mouth with my hand, and staring at Jay lying in bed not moving. We were both completely naked, so I already knew what it was. I mean it was no way possible for him to be there in my bed with me like that and absolutely not touch me.

I ran to the shower, and tears rolled down my face as I stood in the shower with all kind of thoughts rushing my brain, including how in the world did I let this happen. How did I allow myself to get so out of control that I put myself in this dangerous situation. Should I be grateful to be alive? Should I be grateful that it is Jay and not some stranger? Should I blame myself or blame Jay? Is it my fault? Did we really have sex? What kind of sex did we have? Am I okay? Could I have aids or another sexually transmitted disease now? What are people gonna say? What are people at work gonna think? Will he tell anyone? Maybe nothing happened? Oh God will never forgive me for this, right? I had made a vow to celibacy and had kept it for over a year. The thoughts and questions and condemnation flooded my mind and my heart was broken; I was afraid. I did not even want to go back in the room and face Jay. I just wanted this night to have never happened. Maybe it was a nightmare and I will be waking up soon. But no, it was not a dream. It was real. This really has happened.

So, as I am getting dressed I started to notice that I am now feeling sicker than I did the night before. This is called a hangover. My head was throbbing, and I could not walk straight. All I wanted to do is lie down, and bury my head under the covers and forget that the previous night ever happened. I wanted to turn back the hands of time, and erase ever going out to that club, but of course that can never happen. I believe Jay spoke to me first. He lied to me and said that nothing happened. Of course I looked at him like he was crazy; yeah right. Then, he says to me that he will never tell anyone at work or anything; that it would be our secret. In the words of one famous comedian, I was like "Nigga pleeeeeaaase."

For months we fought and argued about that night, as a matter of fact we disagree to this day because Jay has convinced himself to believe that I was not as drunk as I claimed, and know every detail and asked for everything that happened that night. My thing is, when YOU are sober enough to drive someone home; when YOU know the other person is drunk out of their mind, then YOU should be respectful and responsible enough to at least wait until the person sobers up to engage in doing anything to or with that person. Anything else is a violation. Who was at fault? Was he wrong? Was I to blame? I know you have probably had to deal with asking yourself the same questions, or having the same walk of shame after an experience like this. And we are so dumb to let the same so called friends convince us to do this night after night; week after week; year after year. For what? It gives us nothing but a bad reputation.

The day afterwards I drove Jay home. Then I met up with my hanging buddies at one of their homes cookout we had all planned. I remember Jay telling me that he would call me later, acting like we had both had a good time. Anyway, when I get to the cookout, of course there were quite a few people there including Linda and Sheryl. Sheryl was giggling saying, "Niecy what you been into girl." I was like what in the world does she think this is. My reply was, "Please I do not even want to talk about it." Everyone seemed to have been anticipating my arrival because they had been talking about Jay taking me home. It was like everyone already knew that he had stayed the whole night at my place. I was so upset, and embarrassed. It was not what I wanted. I had been saving myself, and even though Jay was my crush, I wanted us to get to know each other first before anything like this happened. Most of all I definitely did not want the whole world to know that I had been naked with Jay.

I was having crying spells, and still sort of shaken up. One of the craziest guys in the bunch started saying to me, "Basically, Niecy, he raped you." Everyone saw how upset I was. All I could do is wanna find out if this guy really did not mean me harm or if he was a sick individual that goes around taking advantage of women in that way.

I blamed myself so much that after a while I took all the blame on myself because I made myself believe that if I had never gone to the club and had all those drinks then it would never have happened. If I had never backslid out of the church, and started all this worldly stuff then this would have never happened to me. I thought it is my entire fault.

After counseling, and praying to God for answers, I realize that no matter what if Jay had been a decent man then he never would have wanted to go as far as to have sex with me as drunk as I was. Like I said though, to this day we both disagree and he blames me calling me a fake and liar. Isn't it funny how the enemy tries to turn the wrong he does on you? Oh, but the devil is a liar. Jay was flat wrong, and he knew it. It took him years to confess and apologize to me, but I am grateful he did.

What I am about to tell you next will shock and probably disgust many, but this is what happens to a woman or person who has been abused; a lost soul. What they do to deal with the abuse is try to justify it in some way by acceptance or self-blame. Well, I know you are wondering what happened with Jay and I after that night. Amazingly enough we spoke at work, and both tried to make sense of what had happened that night. Our mutual friend Frank talked to me and convinced me that Jay was remorseful and wanted to make things right. He told me how Jay really liked me, and even though things had happened the way it did he wanted to get to know me better to be friends; that he still had respect for me and cared about how upset I was. In hindsight, I am thinking that both Jay and Frank were afraid that I was gonna cry rape and press charges, so they were trying to defuse the situation. So I gave him the opportunity to become my friend and make up for what had happened by proving he meant me no harm.

Before Frank talked to me about talking to Jay, I remember getting panic attacks every time I would see Jay at work. My whole body would shake, and I would start breathing fast. I started dressing differently and trying to cover up as much as possible. I would sometimes go to the bathroom and cry. All of these emotions, and the panic attacks were beyond my control. Every episode was very debilitating. After all I had gone through, it was like my mind and body was saying I cannot take one more loss or painful experience.

Every time I thought about forgiving Jay, and talking with him I felt better like I needed him to help me through getting over what happened. Well, a couple weeks later I lost my uncle in New Jersey, and he loss an aunt back here in North Carolina. When I got back from New Jersey it was the same day of Jay's aunt's funeral, so I agreed to see him. He came to my place after his aunt's funeral and we sat in the living room floor and talked. Then it starts. It was the first time we had taken the time to talk since that night. Right there in the living room we went at it like there was no tomorrow. He told me how sorry he was and that he cared about me, and he wanted me to be okay. It just seemed like the right thing to do; what I needed. This night created what seemed like an unbreakable bond between Jay and I. This proved to be just another foot hole allowing Satan to ride me, and add even more guilt, sin, and pain to my life. I am telling the truth, so you can tell the truth and we both can shame the devil.

From that day forward we became inseparable. We had lunch together and even shot hooky from work at his place when possible; trying to be as discreet as possible because we really wanted to become friends first and get to know each other better. We text, talked, and saw each other every chance we got; day and night. He had an affectionate and sexy way of asking me to come to his desk at work, or to meet at his place for lunch. We had the best time together, and became best friends. Soon he introduced me to his friends, but then we had also discovered two challenges that could become obstacles. See we had almost a ten year age difference, and he had no children. To me, it was an over rated experience seeing that whether I was married or single both fathers of my two children did little or nothing emotionally or financially to co-parent with me, so having at least a piece of male companionship in my life was what I thought I needed.

Well 2008, 2009, 2010 went by. Still Jay and I was not officially a couple. As a matter of fact, I began to catch him with so many women that it began to break my heart. That's what happens when you are playing on the devil's territory. Finally, I decided to seriously date someone, but Jay was so super jealous. He watched my every move. I'm not going to go into details about what all Jay did, but it did include showing up to my home unannounced. Once he even climbed up to my second floor apartment onto my patio outside my bedroom. And he always kept his phone locked, but would look through mine. Ladies, these are some of the signs that you are in a toxic or unhealthy relationship with a controlling or abusive cheater. Friends or more this is not good behaviors to endure. At first, it really did not bother me much, but after he asked me to become his woman little by little it began to bother me.

Yeah, I learned that Jay was definitely a player, and on top of his game. He kept me so busy being mesmerized by his charm that most of the time I either forgot to question things, or let it go. Plus, he kept me drunk. Almost every night we spent together we were drinking. I guess that's how we because such a soul tie. We were so compatible physically that we both were mind blown. We seemed like such a perfect fit, but then eventually I realized that this guy had so much control over my life. He tried to bring me down. And I was letting him. On top of that, this relationship was keeping me away from God.

Everything I was pursuing in my life he would put me down about, but I just kept pushing forward. He told me I was too old to be going to college, and that I should stop spending money investing in my business. I mean he just did not support anything I did. Eventually, I started feeling like he just held on to me so no one else could get me. You ever been with a man like that? If I can't have you then nobody can type of personality? Also, I began to feel like I meant nothing more than a piece of meat or a play thing to him; that he didn't take me seriously.

A whole lot of women reading this book have suffered through this same nightmare that I did with Jay. This book is an eye opener for you, and to help you know that you are one of millions of women who have experienced such usury. It is time for you to face the truth, and take back control of your life. Get with God, by hearing the word more and more. I am a witness God will deliver you and heal your heart.

Anyway, I started telling Jay how I felt, and that if he didn't stop mistreating me that we were going to be through. Sometimes he seemed concerned. Sometimes he didn't seem to give a care at all. In the end, this ended up being his attitude most of the time. I just sat by and watch him say and do whatever he wanted, whenever he wanted, and with whomever he wanted while he put rules and demands and ultimatums on me. Have you ever been there? It is like this huge tug of war, but he kept telling you that you will never part, and how much he loves you; yeah right! Boy, the devil can really do a number on you when you give him control. It was not Jay that was pulling my strings, but Satan using him. Remember, the bible says we wrestle no with flesh and blood, so it is not the person we should blame or be mad at. It is Satan that we need to speak God's word against, and command that he backs off and gets out of our life!

Jay said he loved me, but his actions said he did not love me at all. He was just like any other common play. This sick twisted finite knowledge that I had at this point in my life did not come from a wise woman or a father figure sitting me down and teaching me the facts of life. This jacked up way of convincing myself that I was in a loving relationship was a product of the ignorance that I had towards God's love, and loving myself.

While growing up the church taught me that being punished for what God thought was wrong with me is God's love; therefore, being punished for what others thought was wrong with me was love also. As I grew older, and began to read the bible for myself, I grew more knowledgeable and wiser. This is not love at all. I know someone reading this right now has experienced this, and you need to know that true love is not like this at all. God's true love is healthy love. It does not hurt or harm you at all. On top of that, no matter what Satan tries to makes you think bad about yourself and your situation, God loves you. God hates the sin we do, but would never hate us. God does not punish us, or scold us for what we have done wrong to show us He loves us. As a matter of fact, God does not punish us at all. What happens to us, I mean the bad things and heartbreak, are all a result of us reaping from our own actions and decisions. God sent Jesus because He loved us, and Jesus is Love. He will never stop loving us.

The bible explicitly explains in detail what LOVE is. *1 Corinthians 13:4-6 "Love suffereth long, and is kind; love envieth not; love vaunteth not itself; is not puffed up. Doth not behave itself unseemly, seeketh not her own, is not easily provoked, thinketh no evil; Rejoiceth not in iniquity, but rejoiceth in the truth; Beareth al things, believeth all things, hopeth all things, endureth all things. Love never fails."* If someone says they love you then you can tell if it is true love when they exemplify these characteristics. Now, because we are human and have bad experiences and poor guidance growing up, this may taint our love radar; causing us to see or show little or none of these characteristics. I am a true believer that **we all are capable of loving ourselves and others the way God has intended us to, but the only way is**

for us to be BORN AGAIN of the Holy Spirit. *John 3:3*

"Jesus answered and said unto him, Verily, verily, I say unto thee, Except a man be born again, he cannot see the kingdom of God." We must be born again. See, the enemy knows that he can continue to bind us where we are, holding us in what seems like an unending vicious cycle of being abused, and living beneath our privileges. Once we are born again, we find hope in God which increases our faith. We even are more receptive of the truth that we deserve better, and are worth more than that toxic stuff we have allowed ourselves to put up with for far too long. The more our faith is increased, the more our lives blossom into favor, love, and super abundance the way God intended us to have. How do we get such favor, love, and abundance? Through hearing, knowing, speaking, and studying the word of God. Ask me how do I know? Well, I know because the life I have now is filled with faith, favor, joy, love, and super abundance. Why? Because

once God allowed a preacher to teach me this principle, and I applied this revelation, all that God has designed for my life began to unfold and manifest in a great way in my life.

There is Hope

Dealing with all these dysfunctional relationships had me bound up in a place of self hatred and abuse. Being in a relationship with Jay, caused me to war within myself about my self-worth, my capabilities, and even if I could ever be truly loved. I had such a battle in my mind with deciding if I should trust him, hate him, love him, forgive him, not give up on him. Why do we do that as women? Why do we get ourselves helmed up in a relationship with some man who we know is starting out wrong with us, then once their true nature and intentions are revealed (even more) we become self sacrificing, blaming ourselves for what they are doing to us? Why do we try to trust, love, forgive, and not give up on a man who is not trying to do the same for us? The answer to this is, we do this because we were never taught what true love is. We then go through life trying to figure it out without God. To add pain to injury, because we have never experienced true love from both our parents, or more importantly have not learned and experienced God's love, we are lost. We just don't know what love is, and until we first find God's love and allow God's love in our lives then we will never know how to recognize true love from a person, and will always be stuck on this painful roller coaster ride of failed relationships.

What I learned through my experiences and talking with other women is that a woman's intuition is so accurate and strong to the point that a woman should always pay attention and trust it. It's God's love inside of us; screaming for us to pay attention to that little voice. Maya Angelou said it well when she said, "When a person shows you who they are, believe them." This man showed me over and over and over again that either he was all wrong; just like all the other wrong relationships I had. You or someone you know is going through the same thing. Personally, I believe any person who tries to live a lie or double life has real psychological issues. If you call yourself grown and mature, then you should not play around with a person's mind or feelings. Then again, real grown folks don't play dangerous games like that. But there are so many walking around in an adult body, but not fully grown up.

Getting back to the story, it was not until I took a semester off from college in 2014 when I was able to truly see and recognize the signs that our relationship, Jay and I, was in trouble and possible all a lie. Spending time together went from five to six days per week to no weekends at all. So I found myself constantly complaining about it. I mean I complained about just about everything he said and did, and vice versa. It was bad enough that he moved out of his apartment to his mom's house instead of with me, but all the other changes just became unbearable. When you are with someone and one of you, or even both of you, seem to always have an issue with the other, this is a sure sign that your relationship is in trouble or not to be.

There was a time that Jay craved my presence, and we had so much fun together. Then after years of staying in the same predictable state, he seemed to become so agitated with my presence; like he did not like me at all. One thing he complained about is as a single parent I struggled financially trying to make sure my child grows up in a safe and productive environment. I was determined to make sure my son had the best quality of life because I am one who believes that it is not a child's fault that they are born out of wedlock; therefore, a single parent should try with all his or her might to afford the child the best home, best schools, best neighborhood, and best social activities. For those who don't know let me tell you IT'S NOT EASY, but well worth it. Knowing that your child can play outside, ride the school bus, attend school all without being in fear of being bullied or attached or tempted by drugs or gangs is the best gift a parent can give to their child.

I have never regretted sacrificing for my son to have the best advantages in his childhood. Of course, I can never take the credit because it is because of God keeping His promise to me that He would provide for my baby from day one, and from day one God has so graciously done just that. I mean, through it all, I have truly learned to lean and depend on God for every single thing. We have gone through evictions, no electrical power, and repossessions; you name it we have experienced it. But God never left us alone for one minute. There were times when I could not see my way, but just when I was about to give up God made opened up a door and made a way. This is why I will never leave God. This is why you should never leave God. This is why you are not going to give up.

Deep down inside, I knew Jay's love for me was tainted and impure because when I went through a tough situations and needed him, he kicked me down more than giving me a hand up. I remember needing to buy a new car and how badly he treated me. See, I had fear of buying another car because I had gotten burned with two lemons, so I got the bright idea to rent a car for a year. Then I decided to save that money for two months for a down payment on a new car. Boy was Jay frustrated by this. I just did not understand his behavior. He argued that me going to school, and needing his car for two months was a big inconvenience. He allowed me to use his car while he was at work, but cussed and fussed every single day about it. Sometimes, it was so bad until I would cry and just go on and walk wherever I needed to go. It was either that, or listen to his verbal abuse and put downs. I kept thinking, I just needed to bare it two months; then I would not have to hear his mouth anymore. My feelings would be so hurt sometimes. But just like some of you reading this book, I still loved him and wanted to be with him and claim him as my man. Yet this was not true love, and certainly not God's love. I began to thinking to myself, just like some of you reading this book, "How can someone who loves me do me so bad, and kick me when I am down?"

All Jay could say was, "Even though I fuss about it, you know I am going to do it." Did he think that statement made me feel any better or made his actions okay? My point is why do anything for anyone with an attitude or grudge? Why not consider what you are doing to bless and help them? That it can be you tomorrow? Would you want to be treated how you are treating them? Karma is true; you will reap everything you sow.

Anyway, when I found a car do you know this man would not even help me check it out? Just like the devil. He argued, the car is high maintenance, but the car really was not high maintenance. It was an Acura TL with really low maintenance, and in excellent condition. As long as the oil was changed, and everything else maintenance then you can just get in the car and go. No, the real issue was a spirit of jealousy Jay had about my taste and blessings I had been receiving. He got on my nerves with his fussing and bickering.

Then there was my phone. If I could not pay my cell phone bill, which was only $50 per month, he would pay it. Don't think he did not fuss the whole time because he did. If I was low on food and gas he would give me forty or sixty dollars, but fuss about why he should not have to, and that I must be messing up my money. I mean I could not win for losing with this guy. Here I am a single mom, working and going to school full time trying to make a better life for my son with the man who is supposed to love me making things unbearable. That is not love. Yeah, he always apologized, and explained what a mean person he had been to me, but his behavior would only get better for a short while.

If you are in a relationship like this be encouraged and ask God for the strength to walk away before it is too late. If you choose to stay in it, then I pray that you are sure without a shadow of a doubt that this person is for you. Let me help you out. If you are not married then NO this person is not for you. It does not get better.

THE AWAKENING

2014 was my year of awakening as far as Jay was concerned. This was the year that I had enough of the verbal and emotional abuse. I finally had come to a crossroad. You will also come to a crossroad if you are in a dead end relationship. For years, he had me thinking that I deserved to be treated the way he was treating me, which as bad; and that I was too old to get anything better in a man. He even said to me one day to look at him and look at myself because he could get better. Oh, but he loved me? That is not love. See, when you get tired of being tired then you will stand up for yourself, and make some needed adjustments. If you are being put down, called names, pushed aside, made to feel like you do not matter, threatened, beat down or beat on then I want to take this time to speak to your heart. God never meant for us to live like nor be treated like animals. Do you remember when you were just a little one walking around with a bottle, or being potty trained, or taking a bubble bath? Can your mind go back to where you did not have a care in the world, and your favorite pastime was candy, playing outside, or racing home before the street lights came on? Do you remember when your parent or other family members told you that you were beautiful and that they loved you? Do you remember when you did not have a care in the world? How about playing the game choosing a car as your own as it zoomed by, or planning out your life and how you would be rich or live happily ever after? Then it got real; life happened.

Do you remember when you fell in love for the very first time, or went to your first school dance? Do you remember when you first started out in your current relationship and it was all good? The point is that none of us starts out in life or in a new relationship hoping for the worst. And all that going to church each week, having Sunday dinners, and family prayer was God's way of making sure you were taught the basic principles of God and family. By reading this book I pray that you allow God to take you back in your mind to tap into the God and family foundation that was laid in you. It is a part of your blue print. Just like when the owner is not satisfied with the blue prints from the architect then new one's have to be drawn up. God is our owner, and the Holy Spirit is the architect. That's why you cannot give up or settle with life not being the best God has for you. That's why you cannot rest knowing that you deserve better, and can live better.

I told you before, this book is not for those who are just fine where you are. This is only for those of you reading this book who are no longer satisfied being a second class citizen in your relationships, AND who know there is better, AND who want to get better.

It is amazing how life goes. You start out a little one excited about exploring this world, looking for new discovery and friends. Then one day, BAM! That is when life starts teaching you some tough lessons. Some mommy and daddy may have been able to warn you about. Many no one could ever warn you about. As a matter of fact, getting to know mom and dad and family takes on a whole new meaning when you begin to learn they are less than perfect people; sometimes hurtful people.

My story is based on real life experiences that I had while discovering the lies and truths about dating and men. It is all relatable. It is all real. It is all relevant. It is all needed at this time. Sometimes, I wonder if all those people that we grow up thinking are so perfect or have no problems at all; that if they would have been open, honest, and forthcoming with us about growing up and real life issues if things would have turn out differently. Differently for those of us who really needed much more guidance and Godly counsel. I just wonder if as young girls begin to walk the path of paying attention to boys, is there someone there for each and every one of them to give them guidance today; to show then the way; to help them guard themselves mind, body, and soul against experiences that can bring them to the point of no return.

Innocence lost is sometimes heartbreak gained with pain and resentment which tries to go down to the core of our being, reaching way down to the pit of our souls to set a deep root of bitterness, and give way to deep emotional hurt. Deep emotional hurt that when left unaddressed can turn into ugly byproducts of toxicity such as low self image, depression, mental illness, mental torment, anger, violence, godliness, ignorance, vengefulness, and the list goes on and on. These byproducts are not what God intended us to exemplify. God certainly does not expect for us to allow such a negative and destructive attitude, behaviors, and state of mind to continue to exist in any of us. It is time for us to stop looking at others and start to look at ourselves; the only person we can account for and control. It is time to let go of the past by seeking God for the FULLNESS of forgiveness and healing from it in order to press forward in peace and prosperity. Yes, peace and prosperity is what we all need and want; isn't it? Are you ready for a new life? Are you ready to let go of the things that are really not helping you live a happy life? Then start by taking this journey with me, and let's build on it.

Possible Red Flags
That You May Be Dealing With Mr. Wrong

RED FLAG	POSSIBLE PROBLEMS
10-12 Years Younger	Immaturity, Differences in goals and social activities, inability to commit
Daily White T-Shirts	Recent jail release, drug dealer, or thug
Living with Parents	Momm'a boy, Avoids responsibility, Player, Inability to commit, No Career
Temper Insecurity Drugs/Alcohol	Domestic violence, violent, deep emotional hurt, verbal abuser, toxic, narcissist, bipolar, argumentative, PTSD, etc.
No Church Affiliation Use of Profanity	Spiritual Immaturity, toxicity, Dysfunction, No fatherhood/accountability
Little/No Resources No Time or Money Investment in You	Inability to be a provider, user, player, poor work ethic, immaturity, dependent, no goals, not ready to settle down
Late Night Calling Private/Lock on Phone No Public Dates No Label For You	Dishonesty, No quality time, Picking fights, Being MIA, Too Private, Player, Disrespectful, Wants Booty Call or side chick, Cheater, Married

NOTE: These are only suggested possibilities. Use as a guide to investigate, ask the right questions, heighten your awareness, and make sure you know the man you are dealing with before it is too late. Date with a purpose for marriage, not just enjoyment. Always, seek advice and Christian counsel from a licensed professional.

The King of Glory Shall Come In

In life, we all have many experiences and struggles; some good, some not so good, and some even horrible. What I have found is that through God, all things are possible, and through having a personal relationship with our Lord and Savior Jesus Christ we can all gain the power to take authority over our lives and relationships; the power over our lives to be beautiful, healed and free. Most of us want to find the right one, or the right one to find us. Having the abundance and peace of God in your life is more important than any man or woman could ever be. Inside of us is a God given creative power to make our lives grand and great. You are a child of God, and deserve nothing less than what a child of the King should inherit or receive.

Do you consider yourself a child of the King or a product of a never ending sad story? Even if your story is sad right now how do you want your story to end up? Can you muster up enough strength to at least think about the dreams you once had? If you can dream then you have in you what is necessary to fight to make all of your dreams come true; with God that is. In God there is no failure, and after going through the hassle and hurt of all of the wrong men in my life guess what?..... I finally allowed God to heal me enough to send a man truly made for me. We have an undying love for each other. You know, the kind of love that no matter what the person does you just cannot shake off that feeling of wanting them and wanting to be with them? It is like you cannot imagine them not being in your life; like they were just meant to be a part of your life and whatever it takes to figure out how to make that happen the both of you are willing to go through hell and high water until you reach the end of the drama and land in peace and serenity. Stay tuned to hear all the details and the ups and down of my new found relationship with a man who has an undying love for me. Most of all, take all of these stories in this book and the helpful information. Apply it so that you can make sure that you confirm whether the man you have fallen in love with is the right one or if "He's Not the One."

Send all requests, comments, speaking invitations

in writing by email to

healingbrokenheartsministry.org.

or Call 336-268-5184

Follow me and Subscribe

Facebook: https://www.facebook.com/MsVara

Twitter: https://twitter.com/4MsNiecy

YouTube: https://www.youtube.com/channel/UC3yFTXWCZ-1samJS0xDvjrQ

Made in the USA
Coppell, TX
09 February 2025

45688677R00111